ZEN BIRDING

Archery, Motorcycle Maintenance and now birdwatching. White & Guyette alternate birding anecdotes with commentary on ethics and attitudes in birdwatching, decrying ego-centred listing as against just being with the birds in their, not our, context...The principles are universal, and the book is full of insights into both bird behaviour and human foibles.
Dr Anthony Cheke, co-owner of the Inner Bookshop, Oxford, author of *Lost Land of the Dodo*, and former professional ecologist/ornithologist.

Much of Zen Birding *Is a warning to people who love birds. Don't let that love turn into nothing more than a list, especially as an attempt to solidify the self.*
Andrea Miller, Shambhala Sun

This gentle book on birding is redolent with the spirit of oneness with the Universe that embodies the spirit of Zen Buddhism. Written primarily by the keen birder David White while he was undergoing cancer treatment, to which he eventually succumbed, Zen Birding *was completed by his close friend, Susan Guyette, in loving memory and recognition of his lifelong concern for the avian kind.*

Thoughts on, and descriptions of experiences with, birding follow on relevant excerpts from White's birding notebooks, which he took with him on travels throughout the United States....Zen Birding transcends and transmutes the scientifically trained eye and the piercing analytical view of an objective scientist to the world of art and sensitive appreciation of one's environs.

Zen Birding was written in loving recognition of the needs of birds, and not just of those who watch them. The work emphasizes the

different aspects of Zen belief in relation to birding, and should attract a wide audience, as it appeals both to nature lovers and to those with an awareness of, and an appreciation for, the deeply spiritual aspects of life.
Lois Henderson, Book Pleasures USA

Zen in this book is seen as an approach, a state of mind, rather than the arduous Buddhist practice of just sitting in a temple or retreat. Hence the book is really a meditation on birdwatching ethics and attitudes, an appeal to being with the bird in its own context rather than concentrating on competitive listing or overobjective science. A good reflective read on dark winter evenings.
M.G.Wilson, IBIS Book Reviews

Although this book will appeal directly to birdwatchers the reader interested in contemplative practise will also find some gems here. The book also reminds us of our connectedness with nature and the quiet moments.
Scientific and Medical Network Review

Zen Birding

Zen Birding

David M. White
Susan M. Guyette

BOOKS

Winchester, UK
Washington, USA

First published by O-Books, 2010
O-Books is an imprint of John Hunt Publishing Ltd., Laurel House, Station Approach,
Alresford, Hants, SO24 9JH, UK
office1@o-books.net
www.o-books.com

For distributor details and how to order please visit the 'Ordering' section on our website.

ISBN: 978 1 84694 389 8

OCLC 641500953
Library of Congress Cataloging-in-Publication Data
White, David M. 1944-2007   Guyette, Susan 1947-
Zen Birding: Connect in Nature / David M. White and Susan M. Guyette
1. Birdwatching   2. Zen Buddhism   3. Nature

A CIP catalogue record for this book is available from the British Library.

Design: Stuart Davies

Printed in the UK by CPI Antony Rowe
Printed in the USA by Offset Paperback Mfrs, Inc

O Books operates a distinctive and ethical publishing philosophy in
all areas of our business, from our global network of authors to
production and worldwide distribution.

CONTENTS

To Austin

PROLOGUE

With courage, David White progressed on *Zen Birding* during two years of cancer treatment. The italicized passages and birding stories are from his birding notebooks. He passed away from lung cancer in July of 2007. Wrapped in the warmth of David's words, I completed the book in his memory.

David's dedication to habitat conservation continues through this book. His work as Vice President of the Sangre de Cristo Chapter of the Audubon Society lives on through the David White Memorial Fund for Habitat Conservation. For more information see zenbirding.com.

Susan Guyette
Santa Fe, New Mexico, U.S.A.

INTRODUCTION

"There is no place to seek the mind; it is like the footprints of birds in the sky."
–Zenrin

Spirituality, at depth, is about connectedness. In a natural sense, the connection of essences among living beings or, we might even say, among sentient beings applies to animals and birds and probably trees and wildflowers as well as to people, because even flowers sense the movement of the sun and sense the rotation of the earth around the sun. They're quite aware of the daily and annual rhythms of the planet. They sense these things. So they are sentient.

Zen birding is a journey to greater awareness through watching birds. At the heart of this new perception is a shift from objectifying birds to considering birds as aware beings with whom we share planet Earth. How does a passion for nature turn into compassion? When you shift to conscious birding, you invite a change to a sense of serenity and connection.

Perhaps you are a "Birder," who makes a sport of birding, and invests your energies in compiling lists of birds you have personally seen. Perhaps you are a "birdwatcher," who feeds and watches birds in your backyard. Or, your focus might be the potential scientific contributions of their observations. Whatever reason you might have to engage in the practice of birding, this book will help you open an awareness to deeper meanings.

According to some surveys, watching birds is the second most popular form of recreation in the United States. Millions more people in Europe, North and South America, Asia, South America, Australia, and Africa are also developing a keen interest in birds.

Why do so many people consider themselves "birders" or "birdwatchers?" The reason, perhaps, is because birds are at the pulse of the planet. Birds take us through a portal into a part of our natural world that few ever see, much less truly appreciate. Self-awareness expands. Entering the natural world is the cure for the common disconnect, the alienation of urban or technology-based life.

You can approach Zen birding as an exercise in paying attention or becoming mindful of nature—and in not allowing yourself to become bogged down in *ideas* that hinder your grasp of reality itself. Taking the focus away from self expands possibilities in birding.

Moments of Enlightenment

To many (may be most) people, there is a threshold between being aware of birds and becoming an active birdwatcher. Some liken this to an epiphany. It might also be considered as a moment of enlightenment.

For one man I know, this came when he was a young adult, working as a field biologist in Brazil. Doug Trent was already familiar with birds, but it was a technical sort of familiarity. Identifying birds was "work." But one day as he was helping band birds captured in a mist net, he looked at a Blue-crowned Motmot softly breathing in his hand and was stunned by a realization he could not put into words. He was no longer holding a mere bird in his hands. He was holding a small miracle, a creature that even after its release continued to draw him ever deeper into its own world and the world of its closest biological kin.

Recognizing our kinship with birds and other living creatures requires bringing them into our hearts, not just our minds. Thich Nhat Hanh, in *Teachings on Love*, describes the interconnected and interdependent nature of all things as "interbeing." When we hear birds singing, even if we think we know full well that they are "only" advertising for a mate or defending a territory, we cannot avoid simultaneously sensing the cosmic beauty and spiritual depth of those mundane motives. Mindful birding is the practice of carefully focusing attention.

Seeing and deeply feeling the utter abandon with which birds approach every moment of their lives can, if we allow it, help us overcome our inordinate preoccupation with our own self-interest.

It's okay to want a big "lifelist," or to aspire to being a "power birder." But either of these goals could consume you, control you. The key to maximum fulfillment is to learn why these goals are important to you; by doing this, it will be possible for you to possess the list, instead of it possessing you. Sincere introspection may reveal that aspirations for a big list are grounded in selfishness or egotism, both of which are barriers to true enjoyment of the undertaking.

BEGINNER'S MIND

Zen is derived from the Sanskrit *Dhyana*, which means "meditation." Zen emphasizes the practice of meditation in the attainment of awakening and experiential wisdom. Thus *Zen Birding* seeks the essence, or central character of birding, to reach a new and different level of appreciation.

Meditation is any practice that promotes development of awareness without relying on conscious thought. These practices assist the individual in clearing the mind, heightening awareness, and taking the focus off self. Zen birding, as a spiritual practice, can take you there!

As Zen Master Shunryu Suzuki said, "In the beginner's mind there are many possibilities; in the expert's mind there are few." *Zen Birding* will take the casual as well as the serious watcher of birds to the "beginner's mind" which is crucial to the enjoyment of birding. It will take us back to the time that birds first captured our attention, a place from which we will discover an all new and deeper appreciation of the nature of these wonderful creatures, and a journey forward through which we will gain a heightened awareness of our entire natural world.

Can one achieve enlightenment through birding or attention to birds? Yes. The nonconformist Zen master Ikkyu Sojun (1394-1481) is said to have achieved enlightenment upon hearing the cawing of a crow. Each of the crow's cries signified to Ikkyu a single brief lifetime in endless existence. "Enlightenment" has had very different connotations in Eastern and Western thought. Western "enlightenment" is seen as historical, cultural, and intellectual. Eastern "enlightenment", on the other hand, is timeless/cyclical, individual, and beyond intellect. If you feel you've been enlightened via birding, you probably have. You are the sole arbiter of this; the American Birding Association will not certify you, nor will any other organization or authority.

To many non-birders, birding is an obsessive activity. Even some birders may embrace the notion. Our discussions forming this book posed the question, "what is the difference between passion and obsession?" Obsession is being attached to a particular result, whereas passion is eagerness to invest one's energies in something, regardless of outcome.

Birding can, indeed, become an obsession. It can also be a spiritually creative passion. Zen birding is a conscious effort toward the spiritual – a reflective practice that can lead to a new way of being, a creative passion.

Zen teaches the importance of looking unflinchingly at the real world, but also of sensing that some real things go unsensed. In the words of a famous Zen *koan*, students are encouraged to contemplate the sound of one hand clapping. A more apt *koan* for birders might be to watch for tracks of a bird across the sky. The absence of tracks does not mean that the bird did not fly.

ABOUT BIRDING

The existence of nearly 10,000 species of birds, world-wide, brings to mind the "ten thousand things" that Dogen said can enlighten us, once we forget the self. Yet there are pitfalls; birding easily can lead us into egocentric delusions instead of providing a path of awakening and awareness.

Birding has its historical roots in the science of ornithology, which was concerned early on with enumeration and taxonomic classification of different bird species. Later, with the development of avocational ornithology, geographical and seasonal distribution of birds increased as topics of interest.

The growing numbers of "birdwatchers" diverged in their interests. Aesthetic appreciation of birds in one's backyard or nearby residential environments was adequate for many, but others set out to extend their knowledge of birds to regional, national and international settings. Thus was born a hobbyist orientation among people who preferred to call themselves "birders."

We invite you to accompany us as we examine the divergent habits, activities and behaviors of birdwatchers and birders, to consider how these different approaches affect self-awareness and awareness of the natural world, and experience what this can mean for your own life path..

ZEN BIRDING

Can birding be transformed into Zen birding? If so, how would this be accomplished? Fulfilling personal experiences await the observer with greater observation skills! Imagine the freed up energies of birders, for purposes of education and conservation. A shift can occur, for both individual and group actions.

Some would think that doing a bird census while taking a morning walk is obsessive. Rather, it can be a disciplined way of staying in the moment. It is possible to be at one's Zen best when on a familiar path with familiar birds – here, now – yet open to finding the unexpected.

Meditation is not about finding the self—quite the contrary: it is about finding one's way beyond the self. Meditation is also not about "expanding the mind". It is instead about clearing away clutter created by the mind.

Achieving Zen qualities in birding can be done in spite of yourself.

Literally.

It is ego that prevents one from reaching a Zen state of being. Ego tells us that we don't have time to sit and wait for birds. Ego tells us we've failed when we go somewhere and don't see the bird we'd hoped to see. Ego tells us our life list, state list, or yard list, is not quite as big as it needs to be.

There is some irony in the fact that when the writing of *Zen Birding* began, there was the intention (in a very non-Zen-like argumentative mode!) to present a case against compulsive listing of species seen—yet one result of writing has been a much greater personal interest in listing. Listing is by no means the most important thing in birding—and yet, it has personal rewards and it contributes to understanding birds and their seasonal distribution and to conservation efforts as well.

One birder can easily explain her passion for birds to another. It may be quite enough to see a striking species, even if common; or to mention the sounds of a superb songster, such as a Wood Thrush or Canyon Wren; or to reminisce about witnessing a startling behavior such as the J-shaped courtship dive-and-squeak of an Anna's Hummingbird, or the communal roundup of fish by a group of White Pelicans swimming in a circle. Even a shrug, a raised eyebrow and "Well, how could one not..." can suffice.

But to explain the passion to a non-birder is a challenge of a different order. Certain people, even though there is much in common, remain unable to discern the sensibility beneath feeble attempts to explain birding. It is of course possible that someday some of them will have his or her own moment of epiphany, but there is no guarantee of this. We have come to understand now, at this stage in life, that no one can be persuaded by someone else to have such an experience.

Roger Tory Peterson, the dean of American birding, was himself at a loss when pressed to explain why people are attracted to birds. He once commented on the "superficial rationalization" involved in suggesting the attraction of birds derives from their "color, music, grace, vivacity and that sort of thing." He thought it more fundamental that, for many people, birds symbolize "freedom and escape from restraint." Yet he admitted that even a rudimentary scientific under-standing of birds would show them to be "almost as earth-bound as we are." Describing his career, Peterson said, "What had started as an emotional release has swung over to an intel-lectual pursuit."

At depth, the attraction of birding is not that it satisfies emotional needs, nor that it fulfills intellectual ambitions. Birding does both of these things, but it also does a great deal more. The attraction is, rather, that birding is a *spiritual* practice, in a particular sense of the word. Birding offers an opportunity for participating in a unifying practice.

Zazen, the fundamental practice in Zen, is simply breathing and being mindful of the process. Zen practitioners recognize two basic variations of this: sitting practice or seated meditation, and standing or walking practice. Birding is of course not on a par with these basic practices, which teach us to see our breath as the still point between inner and outer worlds, between self and nonself. Birding, instead, is more akin to practices such as archery. Yet there, the same principle applies. Eugen Herrigel (*Zen and the Art of Archery*) demonstrated how archer and target are one reality. Just so, birder and bird are not isolated separate selves, but mere parts of a larger reality. The practice of Zen birding presents the possibility of enhancing that insight.

"Practice" can seem misleading according to the definition in Western culture; it may culturally imply rehearsal. Zen practice, rather, is the real thing. In Zen, practice implies a regular insight-invoking activity.

Science and religion, which coexist uneasily in Western society, need not be at loggerheads. Science does itself a disservice if it pretends to be capable of answering all meaningful questions. Religion likewise sabotages itself when it dismisses findings of science in favor of pretty myths. To be truly powerful, both science and religion need to change and grow, hand in hand. Truth is more nearly to be found in unity of intellect and emotion, or unity of self and non-self. It is in that elusive place of balance where we become aware that the essences of things are not one way or another.

All birds share a single essence. So, too, do all creatures share one essence with all birds. But this is no reason to ignore the diversity of birds and other creatures. Only by observing the variation among them can you hope to approach an understanding of the essence.

Chapter 1

BEGINNERS AND MASTERS

"The mind of the beginner is empty, free of the habits of the expert, ready to accept, to doubt, and open to all the possibilities."
—Richard Baker, in his introduction to Shunryo Suzuki's *Zen Mind, Beginner's Mind*

Maintaining "beginner's mind" is crucial to the enjoyment of birding. When birds first enter our mind's attention, it is the beginner's mind that is captured. The more we learn, the more expertise we acquire, the more we risk losing the innocence of our beginner's mind.

The beginner is full of questions. Why is this a crane, and that a heron? What is an egret, is it a heron? Why is this a vireo and that a warbler? At first, the beginner's questions may seem frivolous to the more experienced birder. But gradually, a beginner's questions probe deeper and deeper, and become more and more difficult for experienced birders to answer.

The master birder is one who knows that he does not know the answers. A master needs the beginner to continually remind him of this. "Serious" birders often think of themselves as being well on the way to becoming "experts." Perhaps they are on the way, or are already experts in one way or another. But being an expert is not the same as being a master.

The true master is not the one who is an expert, but the one who retains beginner's mind and can thus remind himself that everything he knows is mere childlike knowledge. There are many expert birders. Some may well be masters, although many of them would surely deny it. Rather than seeing yourself as an expert, recognize that you know little. Enjoying that concept immensely may lead to more questions than answers.

Beginner's Mind

For more than ten years, from 1981 to 1992, I led a monthly fieldtrip for Los Angeles Audubon, at the Whittier Narrows Nature Center in eastern L.A. County. From time to time, a fieldtrip chairperson would institute a ranking system, and fieldtrips would be listed on the back page of the Western Tanager as being for "beginning", "intermediate", or "advanced" birders. I steadfastly resisted the attempt to label my Whittier Narrows trip. "Birds are birds," I would say. "We always find birds to satisfy the beginner, we often find intermediate birds, and sometimes we get birds that might excite an advanced birder."

What I did not express was my feeling that the field trip leader need not be the best instructor present. My ideal field trip at Whittier Narrows would have been graced with the presence of one or more of L.A. Audubon's many power birders. They would have listened to beginners' questions, and they would have shared their experience and knowledge with whomever was there that day. They would have instructed the instructor. But that was fantasy.

In reality, no one was fooled by my protests. Everyone knew Whittier Narrows was a beginners' trip, or at most an intermediate trip. The classification hinged on the leader, and I was merely taking people out to the same place, month after month and year after year, primarily with the simple hope of appreciating the changing seasons (birders know that even stereotypically sunny Southern California has very definite seasons). We also witnessed long-term trends, like the increasing presence of Great-tailed Grackles. But we were not targeting difficult groups of birds, like juvenile gulls or Empidonax flycatchers. Everyone knew that if we found an Empid, I would be at an utter loss in distinguishing Hammond's from Dusky based on the relative length of the tail or the projection of the primary feathers.

The experts and power birders stayed away from the Whittier Narrows trip in droves. After we located the first county record Common Ground-Dove in May, 1989, during a scheduled fieldtrip, the experts and power birders—and especially the county-listers among them—flocked over to Whittier Narrows. The bird stayed around for a few days and was widely seen. But it had disappeared by the next monthly fieldtrip, and so did all of the power birders.

I was not the one who found the Common Ground-Dove at Whittier Narrows. Ed Craven, a teen-ager whom I incorrectly assumed to be a rank beginner, spotted the bird and recognized it as something unusual.

"What is this little bird on the ground over here?" he asked. I had my spotting scope trained on a chunky bird, backlit atop a distant clump of mulefat, and through the early morning haze I was straining to see what it was. I glanced perfunctorily at Ed's bird, and said, "It's a Mourning Dove."

I turned back to my own mystery bird, and Ed said, "I don't think so. I was wondering if it might be a Common Ground-Dove."

"They're not found here," I said without even bothering to turn around again. "You'll have to go down to Imperial County to find one of them."

Fortunately, Ed persisted. He started detailing characteristics of the bird, and it was only then that I actually looked. When I did, I realized that he was absolutely right. We all studied the bird through our binoculars, and it stayed put while everyone took a turn looking through the spotting scope. We satiated ourselves on the Ground-Dove, and then, finally, I turned back to look again at the bird I had been studying before.

The haze had lifted a bit in the meanwhile, and I quickly conceded what someone else had already suggested. The bird was a Brown-headed Cowbird—a beginner's bird at Whittier Narrows if ever there was one.

(May, 1989, Whittier Narrows Nature Center)

SENSEI, TEACHER

Japanese for "teacher." *Roshi*—"old teacher"

Sensei literally means "previous in life" or "one who has gone before."

Many birders are prone to classification not only of birds but also of other birders. There are ornithologists (professional and amateur), and then there are birders (some of whom aspire to amateur ornithologist status, and some of whom do not). Among birders, there are "backyard birders" who are attentive mostly to the birds that visit their feeders; there are "birdwatchers" who allegedly have only aesthetic interests in birds, and then there are "birders"—a term sometimes reserved solely for those who keep lists and constantly chase after "new" birds. One possibility is to largely dismiss such schemes, because they serve mostly to separate people whose interests are overwhelmingly held in common. Vocabulary unifies those who watch birds and serves as a basis for teaching each other.

Miscellaneous Birding Vocabulary:

twitcher – someone who actively seeks species to add to a "lifelist" twitching, ticking – checking off species on a list

gripping – getting a new species for one's list

dipping out – missing something you should've seen

power-birding – competing to get the most species in an hour, day, or location

extreme birding – an example is doing the Christmas Bird Count at –30°F

twitchable – countable, i.e., a rarity in an area where it can be counted—having arrived by natural rather than anthropogenic means

There is enough truth to the labeling; however, one must closely seek the commonalities between power birders and plodders such as myself. Many self-styled "serious" birders scoff at those of their colleagues who spend much time watching birds at feeders. One young man boasted to "Bird Chat" members that he would accept no feeder birds on his personal lifelist, because he feels he didn't find them on his own.

IDENTIFICATION

Birders sometimes seem obsessed with identification of birds. By way of example, a birder was pointing out different species of waterfowl on a small pond in northwest Florida to a man with a budding interest in birds, when the man's wife remarked, "I don't care what they are—I'm just enjoying how beautiful they are, and how much fun they're having splashing in the water!"

Seeing beauty is important, and so is seeing birds as creatures in this world. You can discern the joy that all creatures can experience in being alive, and when birding becomes a purely intellectual or egoistic practice, this quality is likely to be missed. Yet to only appreciate birds for their beauty, or for how *they* make *us* feel, is being self-centered. We generally recognize that we cannot relate well to other people without some sense of who they are, and this applies to birds as well.

The late Phoebe Snetsinger wrote "...one of the wonderful aspects of birding is that it is endless." A turning point in Snetsinger's life came in 1981, when she was diagnosed with cancer, with a medical prognosis for three months of good health but death within a year. In 1995, she submitted her worldwide list of 8,040 species to the ABA (American Birding Association) and the Guinness Book of World Records, and then "retired" from listing.

Yet when a very close competitor died, Snetsinger expressed both sorrow, and relief that the race was over and "I can happily go on birding on my own terms while others close in and eventually overtake my record." In her own writing, Snetsinger did not dwell on the competition or on her forerunner status, but her son Thomas wrote in the epilogue to *Birding on Borrowed Time* that the shift allowed her "to slow down and to reconnect with her deep passion for the real fun and challenge in birding: puzzling out a difficult identification, working patiently tease a skulking lifer into view, or just being awed by the diversity, beauty and gaudy spectacle that makes the world of birds what it is."

Perhaps of equal importance is that the shift created more space for expression of her sharing personality. On November 29, 1999, Phoebe was in Madagascar. She had seen her 8,450[th] species, a Red-shouldered Vanga, and her little tour group was on the way from Tulear back to Zombitsy-Vohibasia National Park when the driver fell asleep at the wheel. The vehicle flipped, and Phoebe, who'd been napping on a back seat, was killed instantly. No one else was seriously injured, but Phoebe had been gifted with an oft-expressed wish—that she be granted a "quick death", a sudden finality, rather than the slow and probably painful death foretold by the cancer diagnosis. As her son wrote, Phoebe "...went out ... at the very top of her game". Snetsinger's compassion extended beyond other birders; she was an active supporter of numerous conservation efforts and projects.

There may also be some value in people thinking they are seeing something "special," even if they are not. At least they are noticing the presence of birds.

Swallows at Capistrano

Legend states that the swallows return to Mission San Juan Capistrano, in southern California, on a specific date every year. Far more reliable now are the flocks of tourists who descend on the mission, hoping to see the swallows.

The truth is that Cliff Swallows formerly nested on the walls and arches of the old mission, and when vineyards surrounded the mission, swallows were numerous. Now there are subdivisions in every direction and swallows are few. When there were swallows, it was reliable that they would be back from Mexico by March 19th — and although they were generally back at least three or four weeks before that, no one mentioned it.

For the past few decades, another bird has largely taken the place of the Cliff Swallows. People come to the Mission on the 19th, look around, and see little birds. "Swallows!" They exclaim. Photographers from local television stations focus on them, and the little birds appear on the evening news. The anchorperson beams and announces, "The swallows are back at Capistrano!"

The mission gift shop sells realistically-molded and –painted ceramic figurines of these little birds that are everywhere around the mission, hopping around the sidewalks and courtyards, chirping merrily, and building nests of twigs and grass. The little birds are House Sparrows.

(March 19, 1982, Mission San Juan Capistrano CA)

A little pond in Pensacola, Florida contained Laughing Gulls, American Coots, a pair of Mallards, and a pair of Lesser Scaup. They were a lively group, and quite beautiful. But knowing more about *who* (not *what*) they were gave a wider sense of wonder about them. Laughing Gulls are year-round residents of the Gulf Coast. Coots and Mallards are winter residents, having flown down from somewhere north of the Mason-Dixon line, or west of the Mississippi River. The pair of Scaup were winter visitors who had come from even farther away—probably well up into Canada. They may even have nested along the shores of Hudson Bay. More interesting than the various distances the birds had traveled, to be sharing a small freshwater pond in northwest Florida, is their varied habits. Each species has its own distinct nesting habitat, food preferences, and mating behaviors.

But even these considerations can be nothing more than egocentric curiosity for a watcher; there are other more important reasons for caring about bird identification. Without attention to who they are and their abundance from year to year, there would be no way of knowing when a species is in trouble due to something we humans are doing. Mallards, Coots and Laughing Gulls are doing well, but Scaup numbers have been steadily declining since the 1970s. Reasons for this are still not well understood, but if no one cared to see the difference between Mallards and Scaup, there would be little hope for discovering problems and rectifying them.

Passenger Pigeons and Carolina Parakeets are gone forever, at least in part because too few people were paying attention. Eskimo Curlews may also be extinct, due to lingering effects of early twentieth century market hunting. A handful of possible sightings over the past five decades lends hope that this is not so, but what if more people knew how to distinguish an Eskimo Curlew from its common close relative, the Whimbrel? Might we have been able to identify a small population of survivors, and take crucial steps to protect them? And how important is it to know the difference between Whooping Cranes and other species of white birds such as egrets, Snow Geese and American White Pelicans? Without awareness, it is impossible for us to behave responsibly.

Early ornithologists, including John James Audubon, relied on collection of specimens for identification of birds. Visual identification was considered inadequate, and the tool of choice was a shotgun rather than binoculars. Only with Roger Tory Peterson's field guide and improved optics did collection begin to fall out of favor. Still, it persisted in some quarters. A story, perhaps mythical, is told in southern California regarding a well-respected museum curator who showed up for one of the early pelagic trips carrying his shotgun and hoping to collect albatrosses. Organizers of the pelagic trip refused to allow him on board the boat. More recently, someone collected the first state record Yellow Grosbeak in southern New Mexico—infuriating birders who (because only living birds "count") were thus denied the possibility of adding the bird to their lifelist.

Much has been written on ways of identifying birds. To summarize different systems and strategies would serve no useful purpose here. Yet there are also psychologies of identification and misidentification to be considered. Willingness to be uncertain of an identification is an important skill to cultivate.

Saltmarch Sharp-tailed Sparrow

Can you say "Saltmarsh Sharp-tailed Sparrow" six times, quickly? Perhaps some tongues dance nimbly over sequential sibilants, but not mine.

Nor, it seems, do I easily decipher the subtle fieldmarks of sparrows. At first I dismissed the bird as just another Song Sparrow. But then I looked again, with sudden uncertainty. The breast was streaked, but it had no central spot; the head was rather flattened; the back pattern was different; and then I noticed the fairly faint but definite orange triangle on the face.

That was the moment when my mind quit stumbling over its own preconceptions, and I said to myself, "Lifer! Saltmarsh Sharp-tailed Sparrow!"

(July 19, 2004, Scarborough Marsh ME)

Humility in Birding

Nothing can teach humility quite as well as an unfamiliar bird, well seen but unexpected. Trying to build up my New Mexico state list, I went out yesterday in search of Dickcissels and Cassin's Sparrows. Driving slowly down a back road, I spotted a small sparrow-like bird in a roadside pasture. Could it be a Dickcissel?

The bird flew, and as soon as it perched on a barbed-wire fence, I knew it was not a Dickcissel. But I had no idea what it was. I looked, took notes, looked again, took more notes—but still, I had no idea what I was looking at.

It was not until today, after drawing a picture of the bird and tinting it with colored pencils, and after then looking slowly through more than a half dozen field guides, that I realized the bird could only have been a Grasshopper Sparrow.

Another bird for my state list, alright, and a good one—because the sighting left me feeling more humble than proud of myself.

(June 21, 2005, Maxwell National Wildlife Refuge NM)

The Twin Demons Of Misidentification

There are many "demons of disappointment" in life, and in

birding. Not necessarily conceptualized as supernatural beings, demons are attitudes, beliefs and behaviors that lead us into error and disappointment. *Impatience* is a powerful demon that affects many aspects of our lives—not just our birding success. *Lack of planning* is another demon, and so is *being overly focused* on a particular result. *Expectation* is another demon. To avoid disappointment, it can be replaced with anticipation—which is aware, alert, and open to possibility but not invested in particular outcomes or results.

An interesting pair of demons—so closely related that they may be considered as twins—are the demons of misidentification. These can be called *M'aginā* (imagination) and *N'hibi* (inhibition). Together, they lead us into errors involving (1) identifying a common bird as a rarity, and (2) identifying a rare bird as something common.

Common – Misidentified As Rare	Rare – Misidentified as Common
Ego	Ego
Inattentive	Inattentive
Impatient	Impatient
Optimistic	Pessimistic
Gullible	Dismissive
Accepts what others have said	Jaded
Ignores statistical probability (believes in always being lucky)	Believes in statistical probability (believes only the probable happens)

Desire for a big list	Fear of being wrong
Wanting to be seen as "important"	Fear of being seen as boastful

The Twins are alike in being ego-focused, caring deeply about their own experience and how they are perceived by others. They are inattentive to others (including—though they would heatedly deny it—the birds they watch). They are also inattentive to detail, jumping to conclusions out of the desire to be right. Both of the Twins are highly impatient.

A flash of gray wings –
Empidonax; otherwise,
Migrant mystery.

Early this spring morning, a small gray-brown bird landed in the tree just outside my window. For anyone minimally attentive to birds, it would have been only that—a little brown bird. A female House Finch, maybe, or a Bushtit or a Titmouse. Some birders with short attention spans dismiss a few dozen species of birds as "LBJs: Little Brown Jobs."

I've gotten fairly adept at identifying Empidonax flycatchers by genus. These are diminutive Tyrant Flycatchers of which eleven species occur in the United States. They range from five to six inches in length; all have wingbars, most have slightly peaked heads, and all have sturdy little bills well adapted to flycatching. But to distinguish one species from another is a challenge entirely.

Keeping my eyes on the bird, I reached for my binoculars. But before I could touch them, the bird shrugged and dashed off. It was a one-time visit of about two seconds. This bird was making a brief stop during migration, nothing more.

What had I seen? The size, shape, posture and general attitude of the bird made the Empidonax i.d. quite clear. I had also seen the moderately prominent wingbars and the overall grayish color of the bird, lacking any hint of yellow anywhere. The absence of yellow or warm buffy coloration immediately ruled out Pacific-slope, Cordilleran, Acadian, Yellow-bellied, and Buff-breasted Flycatchers. Only a half-dozen species yet to consider. Range, alone, made it highly unlikely that I would've seen a Least or Alder Flycatcher in Santa Fe.

A Willow Flycatcher? Possible, though I think the bird was slimmer and lighter in color. A migrant can show up in nearly any sort of habitat—but I could only admire the intrepid nature of a Willow Flycatcher who would stray this far from riparian woodland!

Hammond's? Dusky? Both are possible, though neither would stay in habitat like this any longer than necessary. A Hammond's might be heading for the Ponderosa forests of the Jemez Mountains. Dusky would be looking for brushier habitat in mixed forest, but probably fairly near water, perhaps in a side canyon of the Rio Grande.

Gray Flycatcher? Entirely possible. We're located in piñon-juniper woodland, the preferred habitat for the species. I've definitely seen (and heard) them during my morning walks— though they're inclined to stay as far from human habitation as possible, so the Russian Olive outside the studio window was also unlikely habitat for the bird. But this was a bird in migration, so habitat counts for very little.

Gray Flycatcher is, as the name suggests, a very gray species, with little contrast anywhere. That certainly seems to describe what I saw. Still, I know better than succumb to a pronouncement on identification with this little evidence. I would have needed to study the bird in detail—the length and width of its bill, the relative projection of the primary wing feathers beyond the secondaries, and the proportional length of its tail. Even then, the probability is that I would be unable to confidently identify the bird without also hearing its voice.

Empids seldom call during migration and so, in silence, they often preserve the mystery of their identity.

(May 5, 2003, Santa Fe NM)

LISTING AND CHASING

"Big mind and small mind are one. ... In one sense our experiences coming one by one are always fresh and new, but in another sense they are nothing but a continuous or repeated unfolding of the one big mind."
—Shunryu Suzuki, "Zen Mind, Beginner's Mind"

Keeping lists of birds seen is a typical and understandable activity of birders. Initially, this is simply a matter of keeping a personal record of what one has seen. There's nothing wrong with listing—listing is fun. While fun should never get in the way of life's important work, self-importance should never be allowed to get in the way of fun.

With certain exceptions, listing is an entirely acceptable activity. In the 1960s, this was quite controversial. Mark Obmascik (*The Big Year*) noted that professional ornithologists considered listing to be "silly, wasteful and demeaning" while Stuart Keith, founder of the American Birding Association, defended it as a sport similar to baseball or bowling, and hence needing no justification.

Still, if listing is all one does, it becomes addictive. To overlook the full potential of the experience, misses the essence or Zen-ness of birding, which is learning to appreciate birds as cohabitants of this planet and as masters of their environments who have much to teach us about harmonious, everyday ordinary life. Listing is, after all, an abstract activity, considerably removed from reality.

Look for ways in which aspirations for a big list are grounded in ignorance, selfishness, or egotism. These are impediments to true enjoyment of your lists.

Letting Go

There were, quite probably, better places I could have gone birding today. Some moderately rare birds had been reported within easy driving distance, and I could have taken the day for myself, perhaps adding a bird or two to my life list, or at least to my state list.

Instead, I went with a birding buddy to a local resort where the manager is interested in developing a bird list with which to educate the guests. We walked around enumerating common species of birds that I've seen dozens of times before, and we talked with the manager, who knows very little about birds, but is interested in learning.

I came away with deep satisfaction, maybe deeper than if I'd gotten a lifer. Sometimes it's better to work on a list that I don't think of as my list.

(June 11, 2005, Santa Fe NM)

Listing can become a "slippery slope" upon which we tumble from creative passion down to destructive obsession. We begin the descent by noticing a species that's missing from our list; at first we "want" to fill in that blank, but the "want" can quickly become a "need" or a "must-see". At this point, we are prone to being mired in disappointment, and the bird we desire becomes an object rather than a living sentient being. Freeing oneself from the tyranny of the list can be an on-going process that heightens the potential of birding; as the late Phoebe Snetsinger wrote, birders "...in general are a perverse lot, often obsessing more about birds missed than relishing the ones seen".

Ask yourself: do I focus on the quantities reflected in my lists? Or do I also pay attention to the qualities of my lists? Numbers easily fall behind other numbers, while qualities can provide us with on-going opportunities for discovery.

Non-birders often ask if listers cheat, claiming to have seen birds that they did not. Birders know this happens, but think it rare. To cheat on one's list is primarily to cheat oneself rather than anyone else. Too, it is more likely to arise from subtle situations—for instance, an identification one initially believed, fully, but later came to question—than from outright deliberate lying. Such situations thus become tests of integrity.

We are, of course, free to keep any sort of list we want, using our own distinctive rules. We can keep a list of birds seen from moving automobiles, a list of birds seen on television or in movies, a list of birds seen on live webcams, or a list of things like leaves, rocks, sticks, blue glass bottles or white plastic jugs that we initially mistook for birds. But even then, we should develop rules for our lists, and we should follow our rules. Otherwise, what's the point?

Non-birders and backyard birders are often mystified, and sometimes miffed, when list-oriented birders comment that a particular bird "doesn't count." What counts and what doesn't depends on the list, the person keeping the list, and the "rules" for the list. Generally speaking, "countability" is determined by American Birding Association (ABA) rules, in order to provide a "level playing field" for birders wishing to compare their lists with the lists of others. Under ABA rules, to be countable or "listable" a bird must be alive, wild and free; seen or heard well enough to ensure correct identification; seen or heard in accordance with the ABA Code of Ethics; seen or heard within the list area; and of a species accepted as naturally occurring within the list area. We are, of course, free to make up our own rules for our personal lists— for instance, counting road-killed birds or birds seen in zoos or on television—but it would be cheating to compare numbers with someone using different rules.

For example, a Bar-headed Goose seen at the Bosque del Apache National Wildlife Refuge in New Mexico didn't count because the species is native to Asia and clearly had not arrived in New Mexico on its own. It had escaped from captivity. Non-birders may see this as devaluing the bird, but that is not the intention. The bird was beautiful and a pleasure to see, regardless of its countability. "Exotic" species do sometimes count, if for example, a census (such as a Christmas Bird Count) is being taken and the species is in the process of establishing a population in a new area. It is important for scientific purposes to track the expansion of non-native birds.

Although a Zen birder may attempt to follow ABA listing rules, the lists may not be primarily about numbers and not in competition with anyone. The lists can be mnemonics about moments in one's life—moments in some special place on this earth, coming into contact, however briefly, with a unique winged being never encountered before.

If you have relentlessly chased a bird without finding it, pick a likely spot that feels right to you and wait there. Perhaps the bird will come to you. If it does, you will be even more richly rewarded than if you had found the bird by continued chasing. If it does not, you will at least have sat quietly in a good place, meditating on the bird that chose to be elsewhere. (Waiting patiently, you could also find something entirely unexpected.)

Embrace the Unexpected

At the Rio Grande Nature Center, I had my binoculars focused on a brightly plumaged male Wood Duck when a small, rather plain little bird came bobbing into view along the pond's edge. I looked at the densely streaked yellowish flanks and the narrow but prominent eye stripe, and realized it was a Northern Waterthrush – an uncommon bird anywhere in New Mexico. This was the first I've ever seen in the state. I had to laugh – a "state list bird" without even having to move my binoculars!

(September 25, 2004, Albuquerque NM)

Whether or not we chase rare birds may not be the key question—but rather whether or not we are mindful in the process of chasing or not chasing.

When we chase, do we rush to see the bird, "tick" it off our list, and then rush off in search of the next exciting moment? Or do we take time to really see the bird, to notice what it's doing and how it's interacting with people and other birds? Do we reach out to share the bird with other birders and non-birders? If we chase, do we take it as proof that we are "serious" birders? Do we then denigrate people who don't chase as mere "birdwatchers"?

When we elect to not chase, are we resentful of other obligations that prevented us from doing so? Do we cloak ourselves in self-righteous condemnation of others for burning fossil fuel to chase a bird, while we ourselves motor around for equally frivolous reasons?

The real test of mindfulness in chasing may be glimpsed when we chase unsuccessfully. Do we pout? Are we jealous of those who arrived earlier in the morning and saw the bird? Are we angry with the loved one who wanted us to return early in the evening, if that resulted in missing the bird that appeared later? Or can we gracefully accept that the bird's existence, its presence in our corner of the world, is more important than whether or not "I" saw the bird?

OBSERVATION

People sometimes think they look, but don't. Look with an open mind as well as with open eyes.

People share the concept of *Samsara*, or suffering. It is attractive because it represents opinions widely shared, but *Samsara* is dangerous. It can encourage sitting around wishing that things were different, or thinking that they are unlike they actually are. Either of these approaches is unproductive. Being productive requires being observant and rejecting *samsara*.

Improbable Moments

There was an entirely unexpected yard visitor today. I didn't see his (or her) arrival. I just looked out the window, and there, perched in a Russian Olive, was a Yellow-billed Cuckoo. This is a "rare and very local" bird anywhere in the northern part of New Mexico — and, one would think, especially so in parched Piñon-Juniper woodland.

29

The bird stayed for ten minutes (long enough for a couple of photos), moving from one perch to another, silent, looking down at the birdbath beneath the tree, yet ignoring it.

Once again, I was reminded: there are statistical probabilities, and then there are birds. Showing up where they show up, astonishing us if we happen also to be there in that improbable moment, armed with knowledge of what has just appeared before our eyes.

(June 2, 2005, Santa Fe NM)

Meditation is one way of enhancing our observational skills. It helps us get in touch with reality. But that doesn't mean just sitting in a lotus position and doing nothing else. Sitting in the lotus position and meditating is a valid way to calm the mind, attune ourselves to perceiving reality and accepting reality as it is. But then we have to get up and start walking the perception. We must do something with it.

When someone expresses dismay with a common species — especially one of those introduced species often referred to as "junk birds" — show them an aspect of the bird they've never considered. European Starlings and House Sparrows are both beautiful, if we only take time to look at them. They can also teach us much about adaptation.

The aggressive nature of Starlings may be saddening, a behavior that results in them displacing native cavity-nesting species. Yet their adaptive nature can be admired, as well as their ability to live in habitats as diverse as inner cities, suburbs, forests, and seashores. One can only marvel that the Starlings picking through drift lines of seaweed on a central California beach belong to the same species that gathered by the thousands in a roost on the University of Massachusetts campus in Amherst.

If nothing else, we can find amusement in "junk birds," by giving them whimsical yet appropriate new names! Thus some people in England call House Sparrows "Slum

Weavers," while a locally popular name for them in northern Virginia is "Burger Kinglets." A Zen saying is that words are the fog one must see through.

It is one thing to describe, in words, the size, shape and plumage of a bird; it is quite another to see a picture of the bird. Experienced birders often talk about the "giss" of a particular species—that ineffable something about a bird that distinguishes it from another superficially similar species. Yet no representation of a bird equals the experience of seeing and hearing the actual bird—nor does a quick view of a bird measure up to learning its habits, and coming to know how it behaves at different times, in different places. To truly observe a bird, one must look beyond all of this. Indeed, observation may be more effective when it begins with a focus on other than the bird.

Conscious Birding

Often I'm thinking of a bird when it suddenly appears, as if summoned. Yesterday it happened with a Western Scrub-Jay. For the past year, they've been surprisingly scarce in my neighborhood, and I was reflecting on this fact when one burst out of a Piñon tree and flew right in front of me.

My thoughts do not materialize such birds out of thin air. If that were the case, I would promptly sit down and meditate on Ivory-billed Woodpeckers, until I had an ample and indisputable population of them. Then I would start thinking of Dodos, Carolina Parakeets, and Passenger Pigeons.

For better or worse, my thoughts do not sprout wings and take the form of birds. But birds have interesting ways of insinuating themselves into my consciousness. Maybe I've heard a distant call, out of awareness, or that I've received some other subtle signal of a

bird's presence without realizing it. Being aware of a bird, its habitat and habits, primes me to find the bird, if it's in the vicinity.
(June 8, 2004, Santa Fe NM)

For many birders, the first bird of the year takes on extraordinary importance. Some see that first bird as an omen, foretelling the sort of birding year they are going to have. These folks may awaken dreading that the first bird they see or hear will be a European Starling or a House Sparrow—an ominous sign, heralding a year of pedestrian birding. Those who take the matter seriously are careful to be someplace where they can awaken on New Year's Day, certain that they will see "something good."

The first bird of the year can be something like a New Year's resolution, only potentially less ego-centered. Resolutions tend to be focused on what *I* will, or will not, do during the coming year. It is, of course, possible to be very ego-focused in seeking that first bird of the year. You might, for instance, travel somewhere distant, where your first bird would likely be a lifer—unmistakably, an ego-centered action.

On the other hand, you might simply accept the first bird you see as the first bird you see, and you can then look closely to see what this tells you—perhaps, something about observation.

Canyon Towhee

The first birds I saw on January 1st, 2005, were Canyon Towhees—a common bird in northern New Mexico, to be sure, but also a bird full of instructive potential. My years-earlier lifer Canyon Towhee was still known as a "Brown Towhee"—lumped with what later became the California Towhee. I had seen Brown Towhees in California, so my first Canyon Towhee seemed to be just another

Brown Towhee, in New Mexico. I didn't bother to look closely at the bird, which was after all "just another subspecies." It was years later, after the Brown Towhee was split, that I was again in New Mexico. Then, I took a close look and saw that the birds were indeed quite different in appearance—the Canyon Towhee has a reddish cap, and a dark central breast spot.

Not just birders observe birds—birds also observe other birds— and birds observe birders.

Dependent Interaction

I pass by two families of Common Ravens during my morning walk. One nest, near the railroad tracks, is so well hidden that I remain uncertain, more than two months after suspecting its presence, which of three dense Piñons conceals it from view. Yet the Raven parents see me coming from a quarter-mile away, call the alarm, and herd the youngsters away from me.

They know I am not just any human pedestrian. I'm the one who stops and stares at them, and worse, I'm the one with the big shiny eyes that I call binoculars.

I know where the second nest is, and this pair of Ravens gets even more distressed by my presence. They call the alarm, but then one follows me, scolding (perhaps cursing) in an ancient Corvid language until I've left the vicinity.

Today, I saw neither parent, and thought I could sneak a look at the nest, where the brood is spilling over the edges. But I'd no sooner put binoculars to my eyes than I heard a guttural croaking and rapid wing beats coming quickly in my direction.

Ravens adjust their behavior in interaction with those who watch them—posing a quandary for any ornithologist who sets out to do objective, replicable research on their habits.

(June 12th, 2005, Santa Fe NM)

Individual observation is useful, but combined efforts become very powerful. "Citizen science" is of immense and increasing value in the understanding of environmental science in general and of ornithology in particular. Frank Chapman established the Christmas Bird Count (CBC) in 1900, in Manhattan, as an alternative to competitive "side hunt" bird shooting. The National Audubon Society (NAS) now maintains a database of more than a century of CBC observations, and CBC count circles continue to be added—some now in Central and South America.

Adding seasonal breadth to the observations, NAS has more recently launched Project Feeder Watch and the Great Backyard Bird Count, in conjunction with the Cornell Laboratory of Ornithology. Cornell Lab has many other citizen science projects underway, including The Birdhouse Network, Birds in Forested Landscapes, the Golden-winged Warbler Atlas Project, the House Finch Disease Survey, Urban Bird Studies, and PigeonWatch. Perhaps most revolutionary of all the projects is "eBird", a year-round online reporting system by means of which birders can not only record their personal observations but also view information submitted by others.

Efforts such as these hold promise of helping us transcend the limitations of ego-centered observation.

READING

Zen masters have traditionally discounted reading as a valid way of knowing. In some ways this is true, but in other ways it isn't.

Our personal observations alone will not bring us to full appreciation of the birds we see. Nor can we hope to learn all we want to know from a mentor. No one person has seen all species of birds in the world. Even people who have seen several thousand species have very imperfect knowledge of the life histories of most of those species.

North American birds have been observed and studied by ornithologists for a few hundred years now, and today we can reap the benefit of their knowledge by reading, and thus sparing ourselves serious misunderstandings. For many years, male and female Williamson's Sapsuckers were believed to be birds of different species! Similarly, beginning birders may have spent little time reading their field guides, at first thinking that the brightly-colored male House Finch is a different species from his drab mate. Reading makes a difference.

At the same time, reading must be kept in balance with other ways of knowing. Pay attention to what you *see* and *hear*, not just to what is in the books. Birds often look different from the illustrations of them, and sometimes they do unexpected things you wouldn't expect from what you've read. Seeking your own understanding of the reality of birds will serve you better than the abstracted statements of others.

LEARNING

Seen in the larger context, Nirvana, or the ceasing of suffering, can be found in the world all around us. Having a real understanding of the value inherent in the natural world can shift us from the inevitable suffering of the materialistic world (never attaining enough) to a sense of peace from life with those of the natural world. Being in the present is the way to get there.

Thomas Merton, in *Zen and the Birds of Appetite*, shows us how insight attained by meditation is respectful of life. Penetration of the meaning and reality of suffering can be reached with daily reflection. Through conscious awareness from thought turned inward, we can become attentive and moved to act for the protection of all beings against suffering by nonviolence and compassion.

Eating organically to keep pesticides out of the environment or creating habitat in one's backyard are examples of compassionate actions possible for any individual. Small acts by many people create enormous positive benefits for all species, including our own.

In *Beyond Good and Evil*, Nietzsche said that "understanding" is like an umbrella—standing under our familiar concepts, we are protected from the hard rain of reality. Just so, unless we are extraordinarily careful, concepts like "species" can get in the way of appropriately appreciating the reality of birds. Yet this does not excuse us for ignoring the difference between one species and another. Far from it—instead, it suggests the importance of learning what is meant by different concepts of species, gaining an appreciation for subspecies and hybrids, watching for the effects of environmental change, and learning about behavioral changes that lead to genetic change. There are numbers of ideas about what a species is, but the two big current contenders are the biological species concept and phylogenetic species concept (BSC and PSC).

Which concept of species "should" we follow? In a sense, it doesn't matter. The various concepts are ideas that do not directly affect reality. The American Ornithological Union and the American Birding Association follow the BSC. If they were to switch to the PSC, there would be a great many "splits" and many people's bird lists would get much bigger! But this would be a trivial reason to prefer the PSC over the BSC.

A more important reason, and one where our preferred concepts have a chance to shape reality, is that the PSC recognizes a wider range of biodiversity, and thus it might contribute to more inclusive efforts in conservation. As Kenn Kaufman has cautioned, "lumping" of species has the unfortunate potential to cause list-driven birders to ignore subspecific differences.

We should pay attention to subspecies, whether or not they're "countable" as such, simply because subspecies are the real "building blocks" of species diversity. Subspecies represent populations in the process of adaptation to particular circumstances in particular places at particular times. If we are to preserve biodiversity we need to do it largely at the subspecies level.

Chapter 2

SEVEN SKILLS OF BIRDING

"There are many ways up the mountain, but each of us must choose a practice that feels true to his own heart. ... Remember, the practices themselves are only vehicles for you to develop awareness, loving kindness, and compassion on the path toward freedom, a true freedom of spirit."
—Jack Kornfield, *A Path With Heart*

If you choose birding as a spiritual practice, there are a number of skills to enhance the practice. Even if you consider birding a mere hobby and think it foolish to hint a spiritual dimension into it, these skills will be useful. Mastering the skills may or may not lead you to appreciate the spirituality of the practice, but failure to develop them will almost surely reinforce the nagging notion that birding is an inane pastime. Investing your time and learning patience develops the "practice" of birding and increases skill. *Pete Dunne On Bird Watching* is an excellent guide to birding skills.

Birding can wake up the senses. David Abram, in *The Spell of the Sensuous,* points out the dulling effects of endlessly objectifying the human world. To live in the flat dimension, with television or computer screens, decreases use of your senses, diminishing capacity. Not using the senses leads to less perception and a dulling of the senses over time.

To awaken the senses, embrace the perception of sounds, smells, and sight as everyday habits. Walk in nature, hearing natural sounds and bird songs, taking time to smell the natural surroundings, and enjoying a three-dimensional world. Be conscious about using the senses to bring back capability and aliveness.

Gradually restore your senses with daily positive choices to experience the multidimensional and slow your pace long enough to feel. Your energy level will increase dramatically. Waking up the senses through listening enhances hearing. Similarly, the sense of smell, bombarded by daily toxin exposures in our personal environments, can sharpen by detoxifying with walks in the outdoors. Sharpen your ability to notice and see, particularly colors, by observing.

Birding, as a process of connecting to the physical environment, supports becoming sharper in everyday life.

LOOKING

"If you want to see something, open your eyes."
—Shunryo Suzuki

In order to see something, we must look—in the right place, at the right time, in the right way. Some people walk looking down, as if searching for money that someone dropped. Of course, they rarely see birds! They would earn greater returns by looking into the sky, or into trees, or ahead at fields or lawns. Other people see birds but don't notice them. They see a flash of movement, or they look just long enough to recognize a creature that has feathers and wings. But lacking curiosity about what kind of bird they've seen, they choose to cut themselves off from a rich and varied aspect of life.

As Suzuki suggested, the first step in seeing is opening our eyes. But opening our eyes is not enough. We must also open our minds to possibilities. Even when we are aware of birds, and deeply interested in them, we may fail to truly look.

Seeing the Now

On the way from the town of Capulin up to the National Monument, I noted, on my tape recorder, a Western Kingbird, and then another. I had seen the even gray throat, the same color as the breast, but I didn't clearly see the white-edged tail. Then, at the Visitor Center, I bought a checklist, and it identified Cassin's Kingbird as a common resident but Western as a rare transient. So when I stopped to write up my notes, I changed the identification to Cassin's. Later, driving out of the park, I stopped for a closer look at two birds on a fence, and they were clearly Western. I saw not only the uniform gray throat and breast, but the white-edged tail as well. I gave the benefit of doubt to the park biologists who compiled the checklist. These birds were just outside of Monument boundaries, in grassland, whereas the park itself is located in higher elevation woodland. That small difference in habitat could easily make the difference in prevalent species. Nonetheless, what I saw earlier were Western Kingbirds, and what I learned is that a good birder must train to not only look, but to also see, and to rely on what is truly seen rather than what is expected.

(August 2, 2001, Capulin Volcano National Monument NM)

Every devoted birder knows about "birdy" and "unbirdy" days. In any given place, one day is abundant with birds, but the next day they're scarce.

During migration, birds move in waves; by watching weather fronts we can catch migratory "fallouts" that put the birdiest of normal days to shame. Winter fluctuations reflect the search for sparse food supplies. But birdy and unbirdy days in the summer breeding season are more mysterious.

Observer bias plays a key role. Of course, it starts with the birds—for whatever reason—but an unbirdy day quickly engulfs the birder. You become discouraged, stop looking, or go home early. The unbirdy day thus becomes unbirdier still. Or, you might take the relative absence of birds as a challenge and begin looking and listening more intently, seeing more birds, or noticing interesting behaviors among those present. Thus, the unbirdy day becomes less so.

"I am like a pelican of the wilderness: I am like an owl of the desert.
I watch, and am as a sparrow alone upon the house top."
—Psalms 102:6, 7

Sight is not a simple sense; it is not merely two-dimensional, and sometimes it needs a helping hand from other senses. To see, we must learn that there are layers of surfaces, some of which are hidden behind others. Annie Dillard, in *Pilgrim at Tinker Creek*, described an Osage orange tree that cried out to her with the voice of three hundred Red-winged Blackbirds, yet she could see none of them until they flew, a hundred at a time, from the tree, "as if the leaves of the Osage orange had been freed from a spell in the form of red-winged blackbirds."

Looking carefully also has its pitfalls. In the 1960s, Rose-throated Becards—a fairly common species, in Mexico—were discovered nesting near a roadside picnic table in south-eastern Arizona, near the little town of Patagonia. This attracted many birders, who then found other rarities (Five-striped Sparrows, Thick-billed Kingbirds, and others). The apparent diversity of species in the area was undoubtedly an illusion, but it became known as the "Patagonia Picnic Table Effect." The resulting crush of birders resulted in an adjacent creek being fenced off by the property owner. What we see depends on how intently we look.

Expect the Unexpected

Every morning from late summer into fall, walking down the North Fork of Pueblo Canyon in Santa Fe, I would look intently at a stand of sunflowers that stretches from Enebro Road down the dry ravine.

I would see dark shapes that looked like birds. Raising my binoculars to study the birds, I would see only sunflower seed heads.

But did I learn from experience? Did I stop looking?

No. And then one morning I raised my binoculars, and there among the seed heads were a few dozen Pine Siskins, hanging sideways and upside down, extracting sunflower seeds with their sharp little beaks.

Another day, there were Lesser Goldfinches. Once there was a lone Song Sparrow; and today, three House Finches, a bright rosy male and two modest gray-brown females. Each of these treasures, where experience had taught me there were no birds. (Yes, even House Finches are treasures!)

So did I learn from experience?

Yes. My larger experience has taught me that birds love weedy thickets, and that my naked eye is not to be trusted.

Nor, indeed, are binoculars!

There may well be birds where there appear to be none, or where we expect there to be none.

(September 25, 2003, North Fork of Pueblo Canyon, Santa Fe, NM)

Wedge-tailed Shearwaters

Yesterday, Susan and I were walking up the path to the lighthouse at Kilauea Point National Wildlife Refuge when she said "birds!" I looked to the sky, but saw neither albatross nor frigatebird nor booby. "Where?" I asked. "There," she said, pointing into the bushes. I looked up the slope, into a tangle of branches, expecting perhaps a little flock of Japanese White-eyes. Still I saw nothing. "Not up there," Susan said, assessing my gaze, "down here." She pointed again, and I looked down, at the very edge of the path. I was looking into an empty hollow, scooped out in the red volcanic soil. Maybe it was a nest, but it was empty.

But then I looked to the left, and in another earthen nest there was a dark gray, fluffy-headed baby Wedge-tailed Shearwater. To the right, there was another.

Without attention on birds, without looking for them, Susan saw birds where I least expected them—almost underfoot. And not just any birds—Wedge-tailed Shearwaters, rarely to be seen on land! Knowing that the babies were there allowed me to return this morning, to see the adults emerging from their burrows before dawn, just before flying off to spend another day at sea.

(November 22, 2001, Kilauea Point NWR, Kauai HI)

LISTENING

A bird does not sing
Because it has an answer.
It sings because it has a song.
—Chinese proverb

Recent research into bird song is providing complex new understandings. Bird song is not exclusively "hard-wired" into the organism, but is instead learned among some species before hatching. Distinct dialects among subspecies may contribute to eventual speciation. Song functions not only as advertisement for mates and territorial defense, but also as communication between individuals (and sometimes it is even understood between species). And it has aesthetic functions for birds as well as for humans. Ornithologically speaking, avian vocalizations are more distinctive than differences in plumage, and they are increasingly being used to "split" heretofore unitary species into two or more.

Accepting the Obscure

The National Capitol is nothing if not grand—grand boulevards, grand architecture, grand statuary, grand aspirations and assumptions of wealth and political power.

But a young European Starling perches on a café chair near the National Archives, softly singing a whisper song to a stranger who has just fed him a scrap of whole-wheat bread. Is the starling singing out of gratitude or in anticipation of another crumb? Or does he sing for some other reason, not grasped by his human companion?

(October 6, 2004, Washington DC)

Mother ducks begin talking to their babies while they are still in the egg, and they respond. Learning the individual voices of their parents is a key to survival of baby birds.

In 1992, the American Birding Association changed its countability rules so that heard-only birds "count" just as well as those that are seen. The late Phoebe Snetsinger was an outspoken opponent of the shift—partly because of the uncertainty of correctly identifying little-known tropical birds—and many birders objected because they felt one should "get to know" a bird before adding it to their list. The contrary view is that truly getting to know a bird is no simple matter of memorizing its plumages and various calls but also of knowing its kinesics or movement patterns, its daily and seasonal habits, and even its interactions with other species. Both sides of the argument have merit, but both for censusing purposes and for birders with diminished eyesight, audio identification will remain an important skill.

Good birders bird with all of their senses. Being attentive to bird sounds close by and far away is important. Our sense of hearing is every bit as important in birding as our sense of sight, and there are people who bird primarily by ear. There are blind birders who can identify birds by sound that sighted birders simply don't hear because they're so far away, the calls are so distant. Birders don't just go out and look, they listen — and they listen not only to identify the bird, but also to learn something about what the bird is doing.

Listen to the Moment

I am intrigued, sometimes, by hikers — especially in groups. They go up the trail constantly talking and laughing, seeing yet somehow not seeing the environment around them. To see the natural environment, we must also listen to it.

(August 30, 2005, Mount Rainier National Park WA)

To non-birders, many birdcalls sound alike — hence generic terms such as "tweet", "cheep" and "chirp." But these similar-sounding calls are quite distinct, once we begin to listen closely. Without even seeing them, I can hear the one-note calls of birds encountered as I walk the greenbelt path and distinguish House Finches, Cañon Towhees, Chipping Sparrows, Say's Phoebes, Western Bluebirds and Lesser Goldfinches. This requires no special skill — only the willingness to listen, and learn.

STALKING, WAITING

In their eagerness to see birds—lots of birds, of many species—birders may become impatient and focus their efforts on "chasing" birds. Chasing involves finding out from other birders where a "good" bird is being seen and chasing after it. This may be just on the other side of town, or it may be on the other side of the country. Chasing can be gratifying when one finds the bird, or very frustrating, when one does not. Ethical challenges may also arise.

Chasing Illusion

I've arrived in Washington State at a moment when three first-state-record birds are being seen—two of which would be "lifers" for me. But am I rushing off to see them? No.

There's a debate going on here, echoing a debate that has emerged regarding a Red-footed Falcon in Massachusetts. Should we chase, or not? And is it a Red-footed Falcon, or something else?

"Not two!" the Zen masters advise.

They do not mean that we must choose yes or no, black or white, day or night. One-ness (not two-ness) isn't achieved by exclusion, but rather through inclusion.

Should we chase? Yes.

Should we stay home? Yes, again.

It is true, as someone said, that chasing concentrates the efforts of the birding community in one place, so that other rarities undoubtedly go unreported. It is also true that flocking to see the Black-tailed Gull, the Red-necked Stint or the Common Eider (common in Massachusetts, but not in Washington State) broadens each birder's horizons, educates them, opens their eyes to new experiences, and reinforces their appreciation for the diversity of life.

I didn't chase these birds, and I didn't search for rarities elsewhere. Instead, I began settling in at a new temporary home, while keeping up with the sometimes excited and sometimes disappointed reports from those who did.

Red-footed Falcon or Amur Falcon?

Red-necked Stint or Little Stint?

Dozens had been to see these birds before debates erupted regarding their identity. Most of the birders who went had never seen the species before, anywhere. Excitedly, perhaps flushed with pride, those lucky enough to find the birds "ticked them off" their life lists—lifer, first state bird, in the case of the falcon, first North American/ABA Area bird!

But then the experts, those familiar with the species from elsewhere in the world—the native lands of the birds in question—came for a look. Just a moment: look at the wing linings, look at the contrast between throat and breast. Subtle field marks suggest another, closely related, species. Maybe not Red-footed; perhaps Amur. Not Red-necked; Little.

ABA rules say we must correctly identify a bird on our own in order to list it. Broadly interpreted, we're allowed to look back and say, "Oh, I saw that, but didn't realize it was important. I know better now. I agree that it was B, not A, based on what I, too, observed." But changing one's mind based only on what the experts are saying is cheating. Waiting for the state rare bird committee to vote and then agreeing with them is dishonest.

It is a perhaps inconsequential test of integrity: do we keep our lifer, regardless of what we first (or later) thought it was? Do we surrender it, bitterly? Or with grace, being grateful just to have learned a difference of which we formerly had no inkling?

(August 17, 2005, Seattle WA)

47

There are various ways of making such quests more fulfilling, regardless of outcome. Photographer Jim Burns in *Time, Rock, and the River*, has suggested that chasing a rare bird can be a Zen thing if the quest is "an accidental excuse for an accidental pilgrimage." With the place seen as the Holy Grail, seeing the bird becomes a gratuity.

Stalking birds poses dilemmas. It is important that our efforts to see a bird do not cross the line into harassment.

Intrusion

"Pishing" is one of the bad habits a lot of birders get into. It simply refers to making any of a variety of noises, hissy or kissy little sibilant and bilabial (two lip) sounds intended to provoke a hidden bird's curiosity and lure him or her out into the open.

I was once a devoted pisher. Any time I heard a bird I couldn't see within thirty seconds, or even if I hadn't heard any birds lately but thought some should be around, I started pishing. I would start softly, and if that didn't work, I would escalate, getting louder and more insistent until the bird either came out, or left.

The first thing that annoyed me about pishing was when I would be leading a field trip, and one of the trip participants would out-pish me. "The nerve of that guy!" I thought (it was always a guy), "I'm the leader!"

Later, a couple of people had the boldness to suggest to me that it really wasn't a very good thing for anyone to do. I may have honored the complaint at the time, just to be polite, but I didn't get it, and the next time out, I went right back to pishing.

Gradually, I began thinking about what I was doing. By pishing at birds, I was interrupting their activities and provoking reactions from them—reactions not necessarily of curiosity (as we like to think) but also perhaps of fear and apprehension. Particularly during nesting season, pishing began to seem like a potentially dangerous distraction. While a bird is watching me, she's not watching her nest, and it only takes a moment for a predator to snatch an egg or a baby bird.

Sparrows are especially susceptible to pishing, and this morning, momentarily ignoring my on-again off-again resolution to stop, I pished a Lincoln's Sparrow out of a blackberry thicket along the Green River. Briefly pleased with myself, I'm now thinking that even during fall migration, a sparrow surely has more important things to do than come out of the brambles to stare at me.

(September 1, 2005, Auburn WA)

Birders have much to learn from *Ninjutsu* — "the art of invisibility" — the **ninja** discipline of stealthy movement. This involves learning to recognize the *suki* or opening. Ninja training teaches 10 styles or techniques of walking, including:

Nuki ashi (stealthy step)
O ashi (big step)
Ko ashi (little step)

Techniques for "invisibility" include taking precautions against throwing a shadow and working downwind to prevent sound from carrying.

Harrassment of Birds

To avoid harassment of birds requires learning something about the birds in general. Some species are very sensitive to human presence while others are not. Circumstances vary (nesting birds are more sensitive). Being *in relationship* with the specific bird in the specific moment, observing what the bird is watching and how the bird is reacting.

Seeing in the Moment

If you've ever stalked a flock of sandpipers, you know the scenario: they're busily feeding, or maybe even dozing off, until you get within good binocular range, and then, suddenly, just as you bring the binoculars to your eyes, off they go—the whole flock of them, skedaddling down the beach, twisting and turning, zigging and zagging, and landing somewhere just far enough that you must debate whether to stalk after them or not.

It was with this in mind that I watched a distant flock on a sandy beach, strung out in a line just above the wash of the surf, as a man and woman walked toward them.

"They'll take off... now!" I said to myself. But they didn't. The couple came closer, and I thought surely the sandpipers would bolt, but still, they didn't. To my amazement, the people walked nonchalantly within ten feet of the closest bird, and the birds ignored them.

"Of course!" I thought. "They're not birders!"

Seriously—it is entirely likely that birds will flee from birders while staying put in the presence of people who ignore them. This isn't a birder's variant of Murphy's Law, but rather a suggestion that birders may give out subtle signals, through our kinesics if nothing else, that identify us to birds as predators. Non-birders, on the other hand, may more often come across as big herbivores who are quite probably harmless.

(August 29, 2005, Kalaloch Beach WA)

Waiting is a seasonal as well as a short-term challenge. Many birders eagerly await spring or fall migrations, as this is when unusual species are more likely to be found. The summer breeding season is often seen by these birders as the "doldrums" because the only birds to be found are common ones in the area. But developing an appreciation for birds as sentient beings, and taking an interest in their daily lives, can go a long way toward curing the doldrums.

Sunrise Birding

There is magic to a rising sun waking the natural world.

I was out birding twenty minutes before dawn on a frosty fall morning in southern Colorado. Steller's Jays were active, Brewer's Blackbirds were chattering as they woke up, and in distant treetops were birds I didn't recognize—although I would recognize later that they were Cedar Waxwings.

I saw no birds before dawn that I didn't see after the sun came up, but it was a special experience nonetheless. Standing quietly at the edge of the Animas River north of Durango, looking to the west, I could feel the earth rolling backward into the coming dawn. The earth's movement on its axis is more easily sensed near sunrise or sunset; slight progress in rotation brings readily observable results.

As the San Juan Mountains rolled toward the sun, sunlight appeared on the ridge beyond the river, and then crept down its slopes. Cottonwoods and alders along the river rolled with the earth, extending their upper branches into the sunlight, then their midsections, and finally their lower trunks. As the earth rolled into the light, birds began awakening in numbers. A few robins were active before sunrise; afterwards, they moved about, excitedly, by the dozens. A male Red-naped Sapsucker posed on a dead branch in a tall cottonwood. Wilson's Warblers searched for insects among willows at the river's edge, and a Belted Kingfisher gave a rattling call while patrolling the river looking for unwary fish.

All of the same birds, and others, were evident later in the morning after it had warmed up. It was not the birds I saw that made the sunrise special; it was waking up with the birds and being keenly aware of being in this particular place at this particular time. Yesterday, I saw the dawn in another place. Tomorrow, dawn may find me somewhere else—and even if not, every new day brings the possibility of birds not seen the day before.

Sunrise birding reminds me of my childhood, when nearly every bird was new. Sunrise birding is like birding in early spring, or in a place one has never before birded. Its special charm lies in novelty and newness. To discover birding at any age is to experience sunrise birding—and no matter when one began birding, this can be recaptured. All we need do is get up before dawn and go out looking for birds.

(September 30, 2004, Great Sand Dunes National Park)

High Noon Birding

Birding at high noon is when we either succumb to boredom, or find new ways of looking at what we've seen already.

Birds need caloric intake early in the morning but get lethargic (and difficult to see) by midday. In any given place, the birds one sees in the first hour after dawn will be the great majority of species one finds during the remainder of the day. More will be seen during the second hour than will be found during the remainder of the morning, and by noon few if any new birds will be found.

One solution is to go someplace, to a different environment. This is the "Big Day" strategy—to spend only as much time in one place to see most of the species there, and then move on. By sampling one place after another, one can keep right on finding new species all day—even at high noon. Or, one can stay put and look in different ways—at various plumages of the birds already seen, or at birds' behaviors, or at something else entirely (for example, butterflies, dragonflies, or wildflowers).

The only special thing about high noon birding is the mere fact of its unremarkable nature. It is a time when we could easily lose interest, or become unconscious of possibilities that continue to surround us. If we do not lose interest, then that is remarkable indeed.

Sunset Birding

Starting a daily walk shortly before sunset provides an instructive contrast with the more usual morning walks. Shadows quickly lengthen, the sun goes down soon afterwards, and bright dusk begins fading to twilight.

Unlike early morning walks, when dim light steadily improves and birds get increasingly easy to identify, failing light requires increased reliance on sound and silhouette for identification. While grumbling to myself about having started out so late in the day, a near-full moon broke through the clouds, prompting me to see the late hour not as a liability but a joyful challenge. Based strictly on tone and pitch of their chips, and a glimpse of their movements in flight, I distinguished a Yellow-rumped Warbler and a Chipping Sparrow, just as the first stars were coming out.
    (*May 10, 2003, Santa Fe, NM*)

BEING IN THE PRESENT

Recognizing and remembering different species of birds, whether by sight or sound, draws us into the present. Birders are more "in the present" and aware of time and place than non-birders, as a general rule, because birders are perceptive about the seasons and changes at different times of the year.

Yet birders could be more in the present if they would rethink the way they value different seasons. North American birders have a tendency to be more attentive to winter birding than summer birding, and highly attentive to spring and fall birding—because these are perceived as the exciting times in birding (if excitement to you means seeing birds you're least likely to see in a given place). It is during migration that birds get disoriented and lost, and birds from the east show up in the west and vice versa. Thus, to see rare and unusual birds in a particular area, spring and fall is the time. A fair amount of wandering and displacement takes place during the winter. The summer in any given place is the time of year when the only birds are resident birds. They're a standard, and if you've birded for more than five or six years in a particular area, you've seen everything that you can reasonably expect to see during the months of June, July and August.

Many birders who are into list-building for their area—whether their backyard, city, county, or state, wherever their birding territory is—have listed everything they can hope to list for their area during those three months. And so during those months there's a particular sort of malaise that strikes birders who are primarily listers, and they refer to the breeding season as "the doldrums", "the boring months," or some other sort of demeaning term, when in truth the breeding months are terribly exciting months. This is when you get to watch the building of nests, courtship and mating, competition for nesting sites between species and between pairs of birds, and the rearing of families. For sheer appreciation of birds, it doesn't get any better than this.

In Santa Fe, we often had young Ladder-backed Woodpeckers during the summer. We loved watching and being with them. The youngster would creep up the trunk of the juniper tree behind the parent, looking confused and not quite knowing what was happening, but inadvertently learning how to find food. Summer can be a terribly exciting time to not necessarily go anywhere, just to stay in one's usual places and be there with the birds, watching them doing the things that are most important to them, raising their families and perpetuating their lineages. This is a crucial way birders can be more in the present.

What about "Big Day" birding? Sometimes undertaken for the sheer sport of it, Big Day birding is more often done in context of fund-raising by competitive teams of birders, in what Pete Dunne (*The Feather Quest*) calls "hit-and-run" birding. Kenn Kaufman notes that Big Day birding provides no time for aesthetics; it is clearly the antithesis of birdwatching. Big Day birders start and finish at or near midnight. They often have a route that they've scouted out ahead of time to find species of birds in an area. Then they go racing breakneck from one place to another. Starting in darkness, they're listening for owls and other birds that call at night. They listen for a few minutes and, if they don't hear the birds, they go racing off to the next spot where they may hear them. They may drive hundreds of miles during the 24-hour period and identify two hundred species of birds, depending on location.

This serves a certain purpose, but as exciting as this sort of birding can be, and despite the fact that the birding may be done in support of good causes, it's not a very contemplative sort of birding. To let all of our birding fall into seeing as many species as we can while racing frantically about from one spot to another, misses an appreciation for the lives of birds and particular ecosystems.

Learn to bird by sitting still in one place. This has been institutionalized in a tongue-in-cheek way by something that people call "the Big Sit," as opposed to "the Big Day." These birders do the same sort of thing — sit for a particular period of time, with a supply of food and drinks for the day. They have to stay within a 17-foot radius, and they see how many species of birds they can see and hear during the day in that one place. Without institutionalizing it, just making this a more normal part of the way you bird, ground yourself and learn to be in a particular place and see what comes to that place.

Haiku For The Seasons
I dreamt of the Spring's
First Barn Swallow, but awoke
With snow on the ground.

USING TECHNOLOGY

"One need not carry the raft on one's head
after crossing the stream."
—*Gautama Buddha*

Technology may seem an odd topic to approach in regard to something presented as a spiritual practice. But a time-honored discourse in Buddhism presents the parable of a man needing to escape danger by crossing a stream. He can succeed by building himself a raft, but once reaching safety, the raft is no longer needed. Helpful, perhaps even essential, but only for a specific and timely purpose. Eventually, it will no longer be needed.

So it is with Zen birding. Technology is a wonderful thing, and there is no reason to avoid it if we can more effectively experience our practice. The Zen archer does not despise the bow and throw his arrows at the target.

Birders now have an incredible array of technology at their disposal. Most essential, perhaps, are binoculars, which birders typically refer to as their "bins" or "binocs." Then there is an array of other equipment: specialized telescopes or "spotting scopes," tripods, cameras, tape recorders and CD players, specialized packs and clothing. An entire "field guide to birding equipment" could be written, although it would require annual (or more frequent) editions to keep up with the latest innovations.

There are also hundreds of books—field guides to birds of the world and to birds of particular continents, countries, and states; guides to particular families such as hummingbirds or sparrows or gulls; and guides to birding locations and what can be found where. Aside from field equipment and books, there are software programs to assist the dedicated birder in keeping up with diverse lists—lifelist, national and regional lists, state lists, year lists, and custom lists.

But as wonderful as birding technology is, and as happy as you may be to use it, a crucial distinction must be kept in mind. The tools of a practice are not the practice itself. Beginners sometimes cannot afford the tools, and the master practitioner may willingly sometimes forego use of the tools.

On Binoculars

As a beginning birder, I did not use binoculars. I came to know Blue Jays, Northern Cardinals and Brown Thrashers with nothing but my own eyes and ears. Even after getting my first field guide to birds, I crept on hands and knees through the azalea bushes in our yard to see my first White-throated Sparrow. The view was closer, and more personal, than I would have again for many years, even with the use of expensive optics.

My first binoculars were, in point of fact, a battered pair of brass binoculars, hand-me-downs from my late ex-father-in-law. I think they were Argentine army issue, probably WWII-era, and although I am uncertain what their power or field of vision was, I would guess 5x. I used them for a couple of years after the rebirth of my interest in birding, and with them I saw my first Rose-breasted Grosbeak and my first Golden-crowned Kinglet (among a few dozen other lifers).

Those were replaced by 7x department-store binocs, and after birding for about five years I bought a modest spotting scope with a 20-60x zoom lens (although the image was always blurry at 60X). For a few years, I birded mostly with a moderately-priced pair of miniature binocs, 8x23, that fit easily into a briefcase.

Very recently, I invested in a high-quality pair of bins—10x42s, waterproof, close-focus, with astonishing light-gathering capabil-

ities and clarity of images. I am grateful to have them. I know I've
seen birds more clearly with them than ever before, and I've been
able to recognize some birds that would have gone unidentified with
lesser equipment.

Even so, I must admit that the White-throated Sparrows I saw
with my naked eye, back in the nineteen-fifties, are as thrilling to
my memory as the Brown-capped Rosy-Finches I saw recently with
the new bins.

(July 25, 2002, Santa Fe, NM)

Some birders will not venture into the field without a full
range of technology on hand—binocs and a spotting scope,
camera, tape recorder, field guide and notebook, at the
minimum. There are advantages to this. One can get good
looks at birds both near and far. It is possible to play recorded
calls and lure a bird closer or even to provoke a hidden and
silent bird into betraying his presence, and one is prepared to
secure photo-documentation and recorded songs or calls of
any rarities that might be encountered. The principal disadvantage might seem to be potential entanglement in a myriad
of straps, cords, zippers and Velcro fasteners! But the greatest
danger lies in the possibility of never seeing the birds that one
has so carefully set out to document. A Zen saying identifies
words as the fog we need to see through, but words are not
the only thing that insinuate themselves between the observer
and observed reality. The more reliant we become on
technology, the thicker the fog becomes.

An American Indian man, a Ute, offered his perspective
about birding. Birding is an okay thing to do, he said, because
it can help you get in touch with this great creation of which
we are a small part. Using binoculars is okay, too, if it helps
you find out who you are looking at. But once you've
identified the bird, once you know who it is, put the binoculars away. "Birds don't like it when you stare at them," he

said. "They think you're being rude."

TEACHING AND TEAMWORK

Zen masters say, "When the student is ready, the teacher will appear." This is true in two distinct ways. A mind in readiness to learn will attract teachers, everywhere, but once one has learned enough, the inner teacher will appear, and proceed to guide the self. It is important to always be both student and teacher. If we begin to think of ourselves as strictly one or the other, we fail ourselves and those around us.

Becoming

Birding can be a joyous solitary pursuit. When first beginning, I found great satisfaction seeing a bird unknown to me, and then pouring through my field guide until I could successfully match a picture with the bird I'd just seen. This approach does not work for everyone. Many fledgling birders lack the self-confidence or patience it requires, and their interest thrives only with the assistance and encouragement of more experienced birders.

(August 2, 2001, Santa Fe, NM)

Recruiting the next generation of birders is essential if we want to engage children in caring about the fate of our natural environment. Many teachers who understand this have started programs in their classes, often sponsored by birding organizations. The Rio Grande Nature Center involved a group of Albuquerque elementary children in identifying a dozen species of birds that migrate from the U.S.A. into

Mexico. This bi-national project included children with some heritage in Mexico. They used artwork and other materials to document their findings. Working together, discovering the behavior of birds that transcends political boundaries, the children accomplished not only increased awareness of politics and the natural world, but also the awareness of the interconnectedness of all life.

School projects can accomplish a great deal, and yet it is also imperative that parents involve their children or grand-children in the outdoors. This is a lot more successful some places than others. Central Audubon in Albuquerque has a lot of younger members, kids ten and twelve years old who are better birders than a lot of people in their fifties and sixties, and they're very enthusiastic and very active. Bird counts and programs are organized by high school students who are very dedicated and very active in contributing a lot to our under-standing of local habitats and the interrelationships in them. Yet, there are other Audubon chapters where younger birders are scarce to non-existent. This is an important topic, posing a significant challenge to those who understand the largely dependent relationship between preserving birds and fostering on-going human interest in birds.

To encourage young people, adults must develop their own interest and awareness. This is often absent, as indicated by a snippet of overheard conversation as a mother and daughter walked past nesting Red-footed Boobies:

Mother (in an exasperated tone of voice): "So now we've seen the red-billed boobies."
  Daughter, early teens: "Those?"
  Mother: "Whatever."

(March 20, 2002, Kilauea Point National Wildlife Refuge, Kauai HI)

The Japanese concept of *toku* can be translated as "virtue," but Philip Sudo said in practice, it means "an unrewarded good deed."

Toku for the field trip or tour leader might include letting a "life bird" of your own escape so that those in your group can see more birds that are "lifers" for them, or in letting members of the group dally watching a bird, or a bird's behavior, that excites them, even if it bores you.

Your unexpected reward might consist of rediscovering what once thrilled you about the bird seen previously.

We often find opportunities to teach, or simply share what we know about birds with interested others.

Birding With the Japanese Ambassador

Last week, the governor of New Mexico called the state Audubon office. Could someone take the Japanese Ambassador and his wife out birding? Yes, of course. The invitation was passed around, and so, along with two other officers of the local Audubon chapter, I hosted the Ambassador this morning.

Before he arrived, we debated—was "konnichiwa" an appropriate greeting or, because it was early morning, should we instead say "Ohayoo gozaimasu"? We had very different ideas about how to pronounce the greetings so we settled for saying, "Good morning, welcome to Santa Fe." The Ambassador responded with greetings in Japanese, and from then on spoke fluent English with us.

We had been a bit nervous about meeting this important person, but there was no reason for concern. Birding brings out our common humanity, with grace and ease. When birding together, we quickly forget about social status, yet we respect one another for interests deeply shared. Still, our individuality comes out. The Ambassador was intent on photographing hummingbirds, while his wife focused on learning the names of various birds new to her.

Before we knew it, the Ambassador was out of film, and we all were out of time. The governor's representative had been disinterested at first, but he ended up fascinated as three species of hummingbirds dueled over the feeders. Upon leaving to take the Ambassador and his wife to the airport, the governor's rep thanked us profusely, as if we'd fulfilled a great patriotic duty.

Perhaps—but it felt like a privilege. Not because we had been birding with a foreign dignitary, but just because we had been able to show two delightful people some interesting birds in this beautiful city of Santa Fe.

(June 22, 2005, Santa Fe NM)

EXCHANGING INFORMATION

Wanting to establish our expertise, wanting ego-strokes, we often strike poses of aloof disinterest. "I've been here so many times before." "I've seen these birds so many times before." "Been there, done that." But this doesn't necessarily accomplish its intended purpose. It makes a claim but doesn't demonstrate it. To really show your expertise, share it. Point out a bird and discuss its fieldmarks or its behavior. Perhaps the person you're talking to will learn something—or perhaps you will. There's always someone with more expertise than you, and it's great to learn something from them. It's also wonderful to be able to teach someone something.

Taking the Focus Off Self

Standard greetings, when birders meet each other on a trail, are "Any good birds?" and "Anything interesting?" I met two birders on the trail around Edmonds Marsh Preserve. "Seen anything interesting?" one asked me.

There are two common answers to such questions—one dismissive, the other creative. I've even been tempted, on occasion to sarcastically respond that the birds were being quite well behaved.

I could have said, "Nah, just the usual suspects." True. I had seen no lifers, no additions to my Washington state list, and nothing worth reporting to the local listserve or hotline. But this is a depressing answer, and worse, it puts distance between the asker and the asked.

This morning, I chose the other answer. I chose to create interest. "Well," I said, "I'm from New Mexico, so pretty much everything is interesting."

Both birders smiled broadly, and I told them some of my highlights: spring plumage Dunlins and Green-winged Teals. They began enumerating theirs: a Marsh Wren and Violet-green Swallows. They suggested that I go over to the waterfront, near the ferry terminal, for Pigeon Guillemots and Rhinoceros Auklets. I added that there were lots of Yellow-rumped Warblers (both Audubon's and Myrtle) at the beginning of the Marsh trail. Both birders brightened again; they had not seen the warblers.

None of us were going to get lifers from this exchange, and probably no state birds. But we all learned about something new at least for the day, and more importantly, we made connection with each other and felt better as a result of our exchange.

(April 24, 2004, Edmonds Marsh Preserve, Edmonds WA)

Teamwork in birding is probably most often thought of in terms of the synergy of a fieldtrip group (the benefit of multiple eyes and ears), Christmas Bird Count team, or "Big Day" team. But the first and greatest opportunity for teamwork undoubtedly exists in seeking out commonalities among the diverse subgroups of "bird people" — who sometimes seem inordinately concerned with typologizing themselves and their peers, considering themselves as "right" or "superior" while dismissing the others as somehow inferior.

The currently favored term is "birder", which often carries a connotation of "lister" or "list-chaser" ("twitcher" in the United Kingdom). Birders, especially men, have rejected the older term "birdwatcher" (and especially "backyard birdwatcher") as a more passive, feminized pursuit that evokes even trite terms such as "bird lover" or "ornithophile". Likewise, people who still consider themselves as "birdwatchers" may dismiss "birders" as "stamp collectors" whose interest in birds is shallow and fleeting. Birders may also exhibit scorn toward professional ornithologists, particularly when they announce splittings or lumpings of species that complicate the accurate keeping of lists. For instance, some birders refer to ornithologists as "ivory tower boys."

There is a fuzzy line, though, between many of these terms. Many self-characterized "birdwatchers" are as knowledgeable of birds as those who call themselves "birders", and many birders have made substantial contributions to ornithological science. "Backyard birdwatchers" make their own unique contributions to the welfare of birds. Feeding birds has become controversial, but using native plants for bird-friendly landscaping supplies valuable habitat. Typologies of bird people create problems in the form of barriers to communication. Rather than seeking out the differences between our own practice and that of others, we would do well to look for what we share.

Thinking Like A Bird

One of the most subtle and powerful skills in birding involves learning to think like a bird. This is at once easier, and harder, than it sounds. One might think it easy, because birds are reputed to be intellectual lightweights. We do not compliment someone by calling them a "birdbrain."

Recent research demonstrates that so-called "primitive" regions of avian brains are sophisticated processing regions similar to those in mammals. These regions carry out important functions, such as sensory processing, motor control and sensorimotor learning, similar to the mammalian neocortex.

Although the level of intelligence among birds may vary, appreciation for the cognitive abilities of birds is recognized as more complex than the assumptions of several years ago. For example, pigeons can memorize up to 725 different visual patterns, and New Caledonian crows make tools out of leaves or human-made materials. Owls show a highly sophisticated capacity for sound localization used during nocturnal hunting, a skill developed through learning.

Planning for the future is a complex skill shown by some bird species. Western Scrub-Jays plan for future needs, catching food in a place in which they have learned that they will be hungry the following morning and also by storing a particular food in a location where that type of food would not be available the next morning. Many species hide food items and dig them up at a later date. This type of memory, called "mental time travel," involves mental images of past events, a difficult cognitive skill.

Sleeping behaviors of birds can be amazing. Mallards are

capable of keeping one brain hemisphere alert while sleeping with the other hemisphere. The brain hemispheres switch off sinking into the slow brain waves of deep sleep. This can be observed, for the wakeful hemisphere's eye remains open and vigilant while the eye of the sleeping hemisphere shuts. Researchers found outer ring birds half-asleep during 32% of snoozing time, compared to 12% for birds in an internal position in the ring.

What we must comprehend is that birds have intelligence of a different order, rather than a lesser amount of intelligence of the same order as ourselves. Respect can come from this understanding.

Archaeopteryx Dreaming?

New imagery techniques have permitted virtual dissection of the skull of Archaeopteryx, the famous half-reptile half-bird fossil creature from Jurassic times. Investigators found a cranium much more bird-like than reptilian, indicating a brain capable of directing the motor skills of flight — and a brain capable of dreaming.

Of what would Archaeopteryx have dreamt? We might imagine that they had nightmares of their predatory relatives, the coelurosaurs, but there are other possibilities. They may have dreamt of conifers, ferns and cycads, among which they perched and hid, or of smaller animals—including little mammals among which were our own ancestors—upon which they fed.

There have been few studies of the dreaming of birds, but some scientists have found strong evidence that birds dream about their own songs. Did Archaeopteryx sing?

To successfully find birds, and to recognize what they are doing, we must train ourselves to think like the birds. With any given species, this may seem relatively straightforward. All we need do is learn the specific habitat, habits and behaviors of that bird, and then look in the appropriate place at the appropriate time. But because we are interested in finding varieties of birds, the task becomes varied, and complex.

Getting stuck in plans versus dealing with immediate reality is probably the most important thing that birds can teach us about the right way to think. Birds would seem to be extraordinarily "planned out" – the more we get to know them, the more we see that they are strictly governed by the seasons (mating, nesting, feeding the young, post-breeding dispersal, migration, etc.), and yet they are also always, everywhere dealing with immediate stimuli. There is both regularity and planning, spontaneity and response, in all that birds do.

Chapter 3

BIRDING WITH MONKEY MIND

"An unskillful thought is one connected with greed, hatred, or delusion. Skillful thoughts, on the other hand, are those connected with generosity, compassion, and wisdom. They are skillful in the sense that they may be used as specific remedies for unskillful thoughts, and thus can assist you toward Liberation."
—Henepola Gunaratana, *Mindfulness in Plain English*

Hanuman, the revered immortal Hindu Monkey God, may seem an unlikely predecessor of the Zen Monkey discussed here. But although best known for his physical strength, ability to fly, divine endurance and extraordinary devotion to those he loves (as told in the Indian epic *Ramayana*), Hanuman was very mischievous as a child. Once when hungry, he mistook the sun for a ripe fruit and attempted to devour it. This may well have come before the more subtle psychology of the Zen Monkey's effort to capture the moon.

This important Zen story tells of a monkey who, roused from his sleep in a tree overlooking a pond, spied a luminous orb and reached out for it. Climbing down to the nether branches of the tree, he leaned over and stretched his arms, trying to grasp the reflection of the moon. But no matter how he tried, his arms were simply too short to reach the object of his desire.

This is the monkey's dilemma: does he keep reaching, until he loses his grip and falls into the water (still without attaining his aspiration), or does he abandon his quest?

The monkey does not distinguish between reality and its reflection, or between what is and is not attainable. Nor does the monkey understand the dangers of desire. Please note, however, that the monkey is not entirely foolish. The light in the reflected moon is real, even if it is not the real moon that the monkey is seeing. Also, it has been observed that human infants sometimes reach directly for the moon—no less a reality just because it is beyond reach.

We cannot *will* ourselves to stop having monkey mind; we will *always* have monkey mind. But we can learn to *see* when we're having monkey mind, and if we become skillful at it, we may be able to become aware of it before we fall into the water. At the very least, we may learn to fall only after deciding that the situation at hand justifies getting wet.

A key to happiness lies in the ability to control monkey mind—unmindful consciousness that scrambles from thought to thought, impelled by negativity and impulsivity.

"Monkey mind" prefers one season over another. We "can't wait" for one season to begin and we tend to fret when the season is drawing to a close. "Monkey mind" is full of expectations, yet doesn't know what to expect.

Expectations

In 1990, I made a trip to south Texas, where one of my "target birds" was the Greater Prairie Chicken. I followed the directions in the James Lane bird-finding guide to the letter. Well before dawn, I turned west onto highway 35 in Tivoli, drove the prescribed miles and tenths of miles, pulled onto the shoulder of the road, and parked. I took a brief nap, awoke, looked out the window, and saw a few shapes moving about in the dim morning light. Picking up my binoculars, I looked and was utterly amazed that I had been able to drive directly to the mating lek. Five male Prairie Chickens were displaying and bluffing one another, sometimes charging each other with heads lowered, sometimes squaring off head to head and jumping into the air. A surprisingly accurate fulfillment of expectations!

(April 14, 1990, South Texas)

Release Expectations

Today I went to a place on Albuquerque's east side, abutting the Sandia Mountains, looking for Cassin's Sparrows. The "New Mexico Bird Finding Guide," a new edition, suggested that the sparrows, as well as Eastern Meadowlarks, might be found in grasslands there. I was surprised to find no sparrows, no meadowlarks, and also, no grasslands. Instead, I found dozens of new houses under construction.

First, I was surprised by predictability; then, by unpredictability. Monkey mind has such a tough time simply seeing what is and is not there!

(June 16, 2004, Albuquerque, New Mexico)

And Release Even More

Thomas Huxley allegedly once said something about the probability that enough monkeys with typewriters, and enough time, would randomly produce all the works of Shakespeare (or perhaps it was the King James Bible).

I sometimes think of this when I see birds that are completely unexpected in a given time and place. Today, staying home even though I would've preferred being out birding, I wandered out in early afternoon to turn off the garden hose (with which I'd been giving our big willow tree a long-awaited drink), when there was a sudden thrashing of large wings up in the willow.

A bird burst out of the tree, and my first thought, judging solely on size and gray color and what is sometimes seen in the willow, was a Great Horned Owl. But then the bird flew around where I could see it, and I realized it was a heron. Then I initially thought, Great Blue?! But upon looking again, I realized the bird was smaller, with faster wingbeats than a Great Blue, and lacking the long trailing legs. It was a Black-Crowned Night Heron, out in the middle of dry, dry piñon-juniper woodland.

A new yard bird, for sure, and a new bird for my Santa Fe County list, as well. And I was nearly as surprised as if I'd found one of Huxley's monkeys up in the willow, pounding on a typewriter.

(May 23, 2004, Santa Fe, New Mexico)

OBSESSION

"Everything dear to us causes pain."
—Gautama Buddha

Obsessions cloud our minds; when we become free of obsession, we are more open to clear mind. Ability to think clearly leaves us free to engage our energies in important issues like preserving habitat, instead of simply focusing on egocentric goals. Obsession puts the focus on self. The central message of Zen birding is taking the focus off oneself and seeing larger contexts.

The Mongolian Plover That Got Away

Tim and Kathy were dedicated birders, single-mindedly focusing their energies on building up a California list that would be the envy of all their friends. They had long since seen all of the resident and regular migrant species found in the state, so adding to the list now necessarily involved chasing rarities. Tim and Kathy were regular participants in the Memorial Day trek to Death Valley, Oasis and Deep

Springs in east-central California, where errant migrants were often found. At other times during the year, they carefully watched weather patterns to see when unexpected species might be found along the southern California coast, or at the south end of the Salton Sea. They also kept in close touch with birders in other parts of the state, and they exchanged information on rare birds as they appeared in one place or another.

Some of their friends were mildly critical of Tim and Kathy for their frequent long drives halfway across the state, or farther, in search of vagrant birds. One person even suggested to them, rather loudly during the cookies-and-punch social gathering at the Audubon Society's evening program, that it would be more environmentally conscious of them to shift their focus—as he had—to amassing a Los Angeles County list. Tim laughed and dismissed his friend's suggestion. "County lists might be okay for someone who can't afford to travel," he said, "but you'd miss a lot of good birds that way."

One Wednesday evening, the phone rang as Tim and Kathy sat having dinner. Tim got up and answered it. "You're kidding!" he said. Kathy put down her fork and listened. She knew from Tim's tone of voice that someone had found something good. Tim went on. "A Mongolian Plover? Where? You saw it? When?" Soon he was back at the table, filling Kathy in on the details. The bird was along the shoreline of Monterey Bay. A friend of theirs from San Jose had learned about it mid-day, from a friend of his in Carmel. He had watched the bird throughout the late afternoon, and he called Tim and Kathy as soon as he got home.

Tim and Kathy were ecstatic about the find. A Mongolian Plover! But as soon as they began making plans, they ran into problems. Tim suggested they leave immediately, so they could make it from the San Fernando Valley up to Monterey by daylight on Thursday. If they promptly found the bird, they could be back home that night, so Tim could get a night's sleep before his presentation at work on Friday. But Kathy had forgotten to tell Tim that she had an important medical appointment on Thursday. She had cancelled it twice already and simply could not miss it again. Tim suggested that he go without her on Thursday, and then take her up on Saturday.

"What if you see it, and then it leaves and I miss it?" Kathy demanded. "No way!" Tim quickly backed down. He was already two species up on her, and he knew it would spell big trouble if he added a third.

They agreed to leave right after work on Friday. Throughout the day on Thursday, and again on Friday, Tim and Kathy fretted about the plover. They talked to their friend Thursday evening, and learned that the bird had remained visible, within a two hundred yard radius, all day. Furthermore, their friend had learned that the bird was actually first seen on Tuesday, so it appeared likely that it would stay a few more days.

Friday afternoon, Tim left work a bit early and drove home. Their birding gear was already in the trunk of the car, so they were ready to roll. They had considered taking Highway 101, but even though it would be shorter, there were more small towns and it seemed more dangerous to drive at night. But traffic was heavy as they drove up Interstate 5, and then there was an accident involving an eighteen-wheeler in Tejon Pass. Tim and Kathy stopped at Gorman for dinner, and they phoned their friend. He assured them that the Mongolian Plover was still there, and he promised to meet them at dawn.

Tim and Kathy drove on, stopping for breakfast at an all-night coffee shop during the wee hours of the morning, and then they drove on to Monterey Bay. They considered getting a motel room, but for a few hours it hardly seemed worthwhile; too, they both worried they might oversleep. At four a.m., they drove into the parking lot, stopped, and napped briefly while sitting in the front seat of the car. Tim awoke when the first faint streaks of daylight appeared in the eastern sky. He nudged Kathy, and they groggily gulped down some coffee from their big thermos and munched a few donuts. Their friend drove up just as they began unloading their scopes and cameras, and he led them to the spot where he had the plover staked out.

The trio set up their scopes and began scanning the mudflats. A flock of peeps whirled past, chattering. When they settled down a hundred yards away, Tim and Kathy trained their binoculars on the flock. "There's a plover with them!" Kathy exclaimed excitedly, recognizing the larger size and distinctive silhouette of the family. "Maybe that's her!" "Or him," Tim chuckled, trying to mask his agitation. "But maybe not. There are at least three plovers in the flock, so my bet is that at least two of them are Semipalmated."

Daylight came slowly. Tim and Kathy and their friend panned their scopes from one plover to the other, trying to see whether or not the birds had complete white collars. If not— if the nape of the neck was grayish-brown like the head and back—that would be their Mongolian Plover. But in the poor light, the birds all looked uniformly dark. Gradually the improving light showed full white collars. Ruefully, Tim and Kathy admitted to themselves that all three birds were the usual, common, to-be-expected, Semipalmated Plovers. Their friend was nonchalant. The bird had been late yesterday, too, he told them. He had not arrived until an hour after dawn, and it was another hour after that before the Mongolian Plover appeared.

Cheered by this bit of news, Tim and Kathy resumed their efforts, scanning flocks of birds in flight and looking up and down the shoreline. By noon, they were getting hungry, but they were afraid to leave. What if the plover showed up while they were gone? Their friend volunteered to drive into town and bring them something to eat, and they agreed to stay and watch for the bird. An hour or so later, their friend returned. He had run into some other birders in town, and they told him they had seen the Mongolian Plover on the other side of the bay, at Moss Landing.

Tim and Kathy quickly piled their gear into their friend's vehicle, and the three of them raced off to Moss Landing. The couple wolfed down their sandwiches as they drove. Weekend traffic was already heavy, and upon arriving at Moss Landing forty-five minutes later, they met a group of people walking toward the parking lot, carrying scopes and binoculars. "Looking for the Mongolian Plover?" one man queried. "It's been down here all morning—left about fifteen minutes ago, so we're going to get some lunch. Don't worry. I'm sure it'll be back. It's been a bit nervous, flying off every now and then, but coming back twenty minutes or a half-hour later."

All afternoon, they waited for the plover. Late in the day, they heard that it had been seen at a public beach farther north along the bayshore. They arrived there at dusk, and could not find the bird. They debated; they decided the bird might stay in that area, or keep moving north, so they took a motel room in Santa Cruz. Early the next morning, they began working their way south, checking the beaches wherever there was public access. They had arrived back at Moss Landing when a birder cheerily asked if they'd seen the Mongolian Plover. It had been back at Monterey all morning, they learned—at the very spot they'd abandoned the day before. They made a mad dash back to that beach, only to hear, once again, that the bird had just left. Tim had an important Monday morning meeting which he knew better than miss, so they reluctantly left and drove most of the night to get back home. They learned from friends that the bird continued to be seen for two more days, but then it disappeared for good. Six months later, Tim and Kathy were still complaining about their miserable trip in search of the elusive Mongolian Plover. Eventually, after a bit of public teasing from some of their peers, they dropped the topic—in public, at least.

Subsequently, more and more birders have equipped themselves with cellular telephones and FRS radios, and this makes it ever more likely that chased birds will indeed be seen by whoever is looking for them. However, this can lead to obsession.

Reflection can lead, for each of us, to discovery of the remedy for obsession.

OBLIVION

"It is nice having a fire, it keeps the room warm, but we do not have to burn ourselves in it."
—Ajahn Sumedho, Teachings of a Buddhist Monk

Sometime in the 1980s, a couple from southern California, devoted or perhaps obsessed birders, decided to travel to Colombia (on their own) for a birding trip.

They bought all the appropriate books; they studied the geography, and they read and re-read the bird guides. They secured detailed maps of the country, and they mapped and re-mapped their itinerary in order to sample diverse habitats and maximize the number of different species of birds they might see. They quickly realized that three weeks in Colombia would hardly be sufficient, but they were determined to make the most of it.

Colombia has more than 1,820 species of birds, more than any other country in the world! Just the names of birds they hoped to see made them giddy: Baudo Oropendola, Black-and-gold Tanager, Blue-knobbed Curassow, Red-bellied

Grackle, and Yellow-eared Parrot!

They bought camping equipment for those remote areas where accommodations might be difficult to find. They packed tablets to purify the water, freeze-dried food, and even equipped themselves with suits of jungle camouflage clothing for better stalking shy species of birds.

So enthusiastic were they, so eager to get in their four-wheel drive rental Willys and head into the jungle, that they wore their camouflage suits on the plane, from Los Angeles to the El Dorado Airport in Bogota.

They got off the plane, made their way to the baggage claim, and were headed for customs. But suddenly, they were surrounded by men in uniforms, members of the CNP, Colombian National Police. Precisely what went wrong is not entirely clear. Obviously, the camouflage suits were a key factor. In a country rife with terrorists and guerrilla groups, camo was automatically suspect.

But it seems other things were involved. His Spanish was a bit better than hers, but it was nonetheless at a beginner's level. He attempted to explain that they were in Colombia to look for *los pajaritas*, but the police seemed uncomprehending. He quickly got annoyed, then agitated, and in rapidly deteriorating Spanish, he demanded to see the commanding officer. His impatience was most likely taken as a sign that something was seriously amiss. The police, already deeply suspicious, glanced at each other and made a quick decision: these strange people must be detained!

Surely drug dealers, smugglers, and if not, they must be deranged! Perhaps, the police speculated, they were deranged drug dealers. Their binoculars, spotting scopes, cameras and tripods were seized, and the variety and apparent expense of the optics aroused further suspicion. Were they planning to sell these things? Or might the optics, or the camping gear, be concealing something they would barter for drugs?

Indignation seems to have been a key problem. A prompt demand that they be allowed to contact the American embassy apparently was taken as further indication that this couple had some seriously deceptive business they were attempting to conceal. Our friends were incarcerated, while the CNP settled into methodically searching their luggage, dismantling the camping equipment and optics in what proved to be a fruitless search for something incriminating.

Things could have been worse. CNP officers were unrelentingly professional in their demeanor. The officers overlooked the birders' outbursts of anger, and there was never the faintest hint of physical mistreatment. Eventually released, several days later, with only the most perfunctory of apologies and without some optics and other gear that had mysteriously disappeared, the birders realized their trip was ruined. Returning to the airport, they took the next available flight back to Los Angeles.

In subsequent years, the pair traveled to several South American countries, but only with birding tour groups. They have not yet returned to Colombia, although the trip is considered from time to time. And no matter where they are going, they never wear camouflage suits.

The incident in Colombia happened before 9/11. Post-9/11, birders and other travelers have necessarily become more aware of human factors.

But even with local travel, a new level of awareness is called for. Business, industrial and military facilities are increasingly sensitive to visitors carrying optical gear, and even if we are on public property adjacent to such places, it will behoove us—and help preserve our access to good birding locations—to not only be aware of potential concerns, but also to respect security concerns even when we know they are not well-founded.

Lessons from Oblivion

*Oblivion does not necessarily involve distant travel. My lifer
Swallow-tailed Kite could have cost me my life, just because I was
paying attention to the bird and not to what was going on around it.
Shortly after noon, I was driving south on Highway 29 when I
spotted a large bird with long pointed wings, circling up ahead of
me. Initially it appeared gull-like, but this seemed unlikely so far
inland. When almost directly under the bird, I saw the deeply forked
black tail and black wings with leading white edges. It was an
instant i.d., but a dangerous one. I was in the right-hand land of the
four-lane highway. I started for the road shoulder. It had not been
recently mown and the grass looked to be about two feet deep. I
glanced in the rearview mirror. There was an eighteen-wheeler
directly behind me, tailgating, and a car in the left lane, farther back,
so I quickly moved left and then further left to a turn lane at the
intersection with Ten Mile Road.*

*I looked up again, saw the bird, verified the identification to
myself, and then whipped through an opening in on-coming traffic
and turned left onto Ten Mile Road. There was nowhere to park, so
I crossed over a double yellow line and parked on the wrong side of
the road. Glancing up, the bird was still there—but by the time I got
the car in parking gear, got unbuckled from the safety belt, and got
out of the car, the bird was nowhere to be seen.*

(July 19, 1991, Hwy. 29 and Ten Mile Road, Pensacola FL)

Oblivion can be a matter of momentary inattentiveness, and
this too can have potentially severe consequences. One birder
told of hiking a steep trail, leaning too far over the edge in a
futile attempt at better views of a bird, then slipping and
falling. Had it not been for the cartoonishly appropriate

placement of a small tree just below the trail, the hapless birder would've tumbled into a deep ravine—perhaps resulting in broken bones, or worse. Being constantly aware of our whereabouts is a very important aspect of being in the moment!

A Bewick's Wren was moving along an embankment and singing briefly atop one Chamisa bush after another. Trying to walk and simultaneously watch the bird, I stepped on a rock and twisted my ankle, not badly, but with enough pain that I had to pause briefly and consider whether to continue walking. Paying attention to birds mustn't mean paying attention *only* to birds.

A remedy for oblivion: research the social, political, and security settings of places where you intend to travel. Become aware of people as well as birds—and of trail hazards—even in your usual birding locations.

EGOTISM AND GREED

"Only those who know when enough is enough
will ever have enough."
—Tao Te Ching

This is a sensitive topic! Greed can be passive, or active. Egotism can cloud satisfaction from birding.

Tri-Colored Blackbirds In Connecticut
In the 1980s, I was with an industry group touring hydroelectric

facilities along the Connecticut River. At one reservoir I was training my binoculars on a flock of Red-winged Blackbirds when Sam, a biologist from Oregon, came over to me and said, "So you're a birdwatcher, eh?" I replied that I was, and he said, puffily, "I gave it a try, back when I was in college. But I got bored with it. I saw six hundred and something species in the first year, and figured, what do you do after that?"

I was momentarily impressed. "Six hundred species in a year?" I queried. "Wow. I've been birding more than ten years, and my lifelist is quite a bit short of six hundred!"

Sam gave me a thinly disguised smirk and asked if he could take a look through my binoculars. I readily agreed and handed them to him. He looked briefly at the Red-wings and said, "Tri-colored Blackbirds. Yep. They've always been one of my favorites."

In that instant, I glimpsed a significant truth about Sam's six hundred species. A bit later, I asked a question that might buttress my suspicions. "Have you done much birding in California?" I asked. Sam said, "No, oddly enough—you'd think, being from the west coast, I would have. But I never made it down to California."

Tri-colored Blackbirds are one of several species that are very nearly endemic to California. Their range extends slightly into Baja California, but they are rarely found elsewhere in the United States. Even in California, they are greatly outnumbered by the closely related Red-winged Blackbirds, and they are found only in a few restricted locations. Red-winged Blackbirds, on the other hand, are abundantly found throughout North America. Even at the time when he first thought he had seen a Tri-colored Blackbird, Sam had not bothered to look at a range map to see if his identification made sense. His impressive lifelist clearly existed mostly in his imagination, and as I got to know him a bit better in subsequent years, I realized it was only one of many things he used to make himself feel competent and important.

Sam's exaggerated claims might better be seen as the egotism of a non-birder. Yet his glib misidentification of a species that would have been three thousand miles out of range is, in a way, typical of some ego-centered birders for whom the lure of ticking another species overcomes all other considerations.

(June 1985, Connecticut River, MA)

In his book *Kingbird Highway*, Kenn Kaufman demonstrates the difficulty of finding six hundred North American species in a year. His discussion of the egotism that may drive an effort of that sort is more implicit than explicit, yet the message is clear, and Kaufman's personal listing effort increasingly became a distraction from other goals. In the end, Kaufman doesn't even claim a precise number seen for the year—it was either 666 or 671, depending on taxonomy—and he commented modestly, but with probable full-truth disclosure, that "I really did not care anymore ... list-chasing had lost most of its appeal for me."

Remedies for egotism: Remember when you made a bad call, and were embarassed in front of others. Step back and consider just how incomprehensible some of your ego-centered birding goals are to non-birders.

DAMAGING HABITAT IN SEARCH OF BIRDS

Surprisingly, U.S. government agencies in charge of habitat preservation have sometimes been guilty of damaging habitat in order to provide better viewing opportunities to birders. For years, the U.S. Fish and Wildlife Service (USFWS) drove an enormous rail buggy through the swamps of Anahuac National Wildlife Refuge in search of Yellow Rails. This was halted in 1988, but then the USFWS allowed birders to line up and drag a weighted rope through the swamp in order to flush the rails.

A remedy for greed: When you can't find the bird you want, show a bird to someone else.

LUCK AND KARMA

There is something to luck—being in the right place at the right time, looking in the right direction at the right moment. We might consider it lucky to be looking to the sky instead of into the bushes when an uncommon raptor silently glides past. At another moment, it might be luck that turns our gaze into a bush behind us, so that we find a rare warbler while others in the group are searching the sky. There is also bad luck, which causes us to miss birds we should have seen; over a long stretch, these may be referred to as nemesis (or jinxed) birds.

But there is also something to karma—seen not necessarily through the lens of ego, which presumes that past lives are our own, but rather through a social and cultural lens, recognizing how our abilities to look and listen are learned from others, abilities that come from their experiences and the experiences of their teachers before them. Likewise, we create karma for others, in what we teach and share. Jean Smith (*The Beginner's Guide to Zen Buddhism*) says karma means that we are what we do.

The ability to find unexpected birds is a matter of accumulated skills, some of which we can easily describe in words and others that are subtle, even ineffable. Do you know the feeling you experience when an unseen person is watching you? Such nearly extrasensory recognition of another being's presence is possible with regard to birds as well as people.

We can train ourselves to be ever more aware of others—of people and of birds. To see the unexpected, we can train ourselves to look in unexpected places, and in unexpected ways. We can train ourselves to listen, ever more carefully, to all the varied sounds of nature, and we can train ourselves to accept fortuities.

Finding Unexpected Birds

Today, after working at the library in town all afternoon, I thought about going birding somewhere I don't usually go.

But I didn't know where to go, so instead I came back home.

Sitting in my studio office, I looked outside and there, at one of the feeders, were two Mountain Chickadees. I see them here with fair regularity during the winter, but in late June?

Would I have found anything this interesting had I taken the other fork?

(June 24, 2005, Santa Fe NM)

Many times, rare birds are unexpected only because birders are unaware of possibilities. Well-educated birders know not only the birds that have previously been seen in a particular area; they also know which birds have not been previously seen, but are likely to wander into the area. Many "first state record" birds are indeed expected, and they are likely to be found by birders who know both the time and the place where they are likely to appear.

We must learn to look in the right direction at the appropriate moment, and to be silent when other voices are directed toward us, if we are to have "luck" in birding.

CALMING THE BIRDER'S MONKEY MIND

What can we birders do to calm our monkey minds? One approach is to meditate on the four *maras*, corruptions or errors of the mind. They include:

Devaputra mara – the pursuit of pleasure.
Klesha mara – using our emotions to avoid awakening to reality.
Skandha mara – the attempt to be who we think we are.
Yama mara – fear of death and fear of life.

Each of the maras seems, at first glance, quite different. What they have in common is susceptibility to illusion and grasping, while avoiding the confrontation with reality.

As mentioned before, tendencies toward monkey mind can be very difficult, perhaps impossible, to banish entirely. One way of dealing with this is through the example of Ikkyu, who became enlightened upon hearing a cawing crow. Ikkyu recommended becoming absorbed in one's desires instead of letting them control one's actions—the so-called "left-hand path". Understanding desire allows it to be controlled. This does not mean simply surrendering to the maras; instead, it requires working with them and becoming aware of our susceptibilities in order to transcend them.

Chapter 4

PATHS TO SPIRITUAL AWARENESS
THROUGH BIRDING

"There is another word for self-discipline. It is patience."
—Henepola Gunaratana, *Mindfulness in Plain English*

Birding can be a spiritual practice. True spirituality is something that has to be nurtured, something that requires practice, but spirituality is about being aware of and participating in the connectedness between sentient beings. One of our key spiritual tasks is to become more aware of these things and live our lives in accordance with what we learn in so doing. In that sense, birding can very definitely be a spiritual practice. Birding becomes a practice whether you participate in it only by feeding the birds that come to your backyard or by taking your practice to greater depths.

People who are "feeder birders" become very attuned to the life that's going on in their backyard, and they become attuned to the needs of those birds for food, shelter and water. There are birders who are much more active and go farther afield. They keep lists and are aware of a wider range of habitats and more species of birds, and that's a good thing, too. But it isn't necessarily a better thing than those people who simply feed birds in their backyard and appreciate them. There are many different spiritual practices that people participate in according to their life situation and their needs.

A common notion is that just sitting and being aware is boring. That notion of what is boring leads us to the accumulation of toys and a materialistic way of life. A different way of being is learning to sit in tune with nature. This is why birding can be very important for children. Currently, few are learning many of the valuable life skills that will enable them to understand relationships in the future, that will enable them to work as a team and know what collaboration is all about, that will enable them to know the slower pace by which nature leads to productivity.

The concept of time that birders have or learn is another important aspect of birding. As we proceed in our Western linear mode of thinking in day-to-day life, planning one event after another, working toward goals, always living for the future, much ongoing perception of life is lost. Birders tend to have, or develop, a similar perception of time as do Native people— that of the cyclical nature of time. Native people learn to live by the seasons and are observant of the cycles that happen in life. The grave danger in linear thinking is losing sight of the cycles of life and the patterns around us.

Detachment without disinterest is the key to being present.

Involvement without obsession is Zen birding.

Developing A Sense Of Kinship With All Living Beings

The notion of human kinship with animals—and plants—is neither romantic drivel nor mere symbolic or mythic truth. It is literal truth. The creatures of this planet are elementally bound together. We are all built of *this* planet's protoplasm.

Birding can help develop an understanding of self that is grounded in everyday life and in relationship with our fellow creatures. As beautiful and mystical as birds may sometimes seem, we cannot closely observe them without realizing their constant involvement in feeding themselves and their families, and in finding mates, providing shelter, and perpetuating themselves through new generations.

So-called "primitive" people have often considered birds sacred precisely because, more than any other sort of living creature, they mediate between, and join together, the various realms of earth, water and sky. Is this merely a metaphoric insight? Or do birds provide literal insight to the relationship of matter and spirit? A well-developed appreciation of birds may lead us to see that this is not a Zen question. Instead of pondering such imponderables, we need to simply spread our wings and fly. Or . . . go watch some birds.

Birders may have a stronger sense of place than most people living in the modern world, a direct result of observing the geographical groundedness of birds. In contemporary society, there is much talk of fostering a "sense of place". Sometimes this is merely a vehicle for asserting proprietary rights. Yet the birder's sense of place is decidedly non-territorial. Getting to know a place by getting to know its birds fosters no illusion of owning the place. On the contrary, what it shows is just how deeply the place owns its creatures. It is the *place* that becomes impoverished when it loses one of its creatures.

OVERCOMING SELF-ABSORPTION

Is birding a self-directed or other-directed activity? It can, in fact, be either, or both. To the extent that we seek birds for the purpose of competitive listing or for other egocentric reasons, it is clearly self-absorbed. There is little in the way of compassion for competitors (although there is often more than might be expected). The focus is on pride in one's own accomplishments. There may also be a lack of compassion for the birds, as well. Shock resulted when a renowned bird photographer announced to an Audubon board meeting that he didn't care whether or not the California Condor went extinct, so long as he had good photos of the species!

Overcoming self-absorption involves doing battle with egotism. Too often, we focus on self instead of the fabric of life. "Creatureness" involves life and death, and being part of the food chain. A Zen perspective does not dismiss any of this. It would instead merge the sense of horror that feeder-birders feel over siskins being picked off by a Sharp-shinned Hawk, with the objective detachment promoted by hard-core birders.

To the extent that we seek to share what we find with others and use our knowledge to further conservation goals, it becomes other-directed. Most birders mix the two approaches. Finding an appropriate sense of balance is key to both self-satisfaction and contributing to others.

Kaizen means "continuous improvement." From a Zen perspective, this entails attention to more than the skills and capabilities of ego. A useful direction for improvement is toward increased caring about, and caring for birds and the earth. An extreme challenge for some who feed birds is extending compassion to squirrels, who raid feeders with such extraordinary competence.

We cannot even come close to fully appreciating a bird without knowing who it is, and something of its natural history. When I first saw Whistling (Tundra) Swans flying through the later winter mists over Round Lake, near Bath, N.Y., I was impressed by their sheer size, beauty, and strength of flight. But little did I know then, they would not reach their breeding grounds until the Arctic islands north of Hudson Bay would thaw. They had flown four thousand miles to their wintering ground on Chesapeake Bay or even farther south. Round Lake was just a brief stop along the way.

Desire is paradoxical. The more intensely we desire

something, the more willing we may become to see it destroyed, or to destroy ourselves in the process of pursuit. This accounts for many murders and suicides. Among birders, it explains why we sometimes trample habitat or put ourselves at great risk in the attempt to see a bird we think we "need."

Surrendering The Palila

Of all the endemics on the Big Island of Hawaii, I most wanted a Palila. For sheer beauty, I might have wanted a scarlet-and-black I'iwi, but I had already seen them quite well on Kauai. For uniqueness, I probably should have given preference to the Akiapolaau, with its short thick straight lower bill and long thin curved upper bill. But I preferred the Palila, less for its physical characteristics than because the Palila is the only bird ever to have successfully sued the state in which it lives. An environmental coalition had filed in the name of the Palila, and that action forced the state of Hawaii to remove feral sheep and goats that were stripping the limited habitat of the legumaceous mamane tree upon which the Palila depends for its existence.

This was Susan's and my tenth anniversary trip. The first hint of a problem came a few days before we departed for Hawaii when I mentioned to my wife that I had completed a plan for my island birding, listing birds I hoped to see and places where I might see them. She asked if I had made an itinerary with our flight numbers, car rental reservation numbers, lodging phone numbers and all of that. I hadn't, and quickly did so. But her next question was unsettling. How much time did I plan to spend birding?

I had not calculated that, but quickly did so. I explained that one day would be set aside for the Saddle Road kipukas, especially the Puu Laau area where the Palila is found. Another day we could spend together at the Hawaiian Volcanoes National Park, although I would be hiking several trails that would be too strenuous for Susan (who was nursing a leg injury). Then there would be at least half a day spent on the leeward side of the island, which is best for migratory waterfowl and many of the introduced species on the island. So—two and a half days. We were arriving on the 5th, and departing on the 12th. I had counted this as six and a half days on the island, considering that we weren't flying out until early afternoon. But Susan pointed out that the departure day would be spent packing up and driving to the airport, and one day would be taken up in the move from one bed & breakfast to another. So was I really planning to spend two and a half days out of five in birding?

After all, we had talked a lot about going to the beach, dining out, and spending afternoons just being together. I had considerable difficulty surrendering the idea of finding a Palila, which is considered by Doug Pratt to be "the only finchlike Hawaiian honeycreeper the average birder is likely to see." But upon reflection (and with a bit more conversation on the topic) it seemed this was the best course of action. The Saddle Road trip would be an all-day undertaking, if I did both Puu Laau and the Puu Oo/Powerline Road trails. Besides, the rental car contract did in fact specify that Saddle Road is a prohibited area. The birding guidebooks to Hawaii admit that there's a risk, but they minimize it, and I had been ready to take my chances.

On the morning of our first day, I got a good view of an I'o, the Hawaiian Hawk found only on the island of Hawaii. Realizing that I would probably find other Big Island endemics at Volcanoes National Park, I relaxed a bit. Clearly, I would not find all of the possible endemics during a one-week visit, so what difference did it really make if I saw a Palila or not? I had already surrendered the possibility of seeing an Alalā, the Hawaiian Crow. Reduced to a wild population of only thirteen birds, located on a large ranch that I then believed inaccessible to the public, the Alalā's survival now depends largely on a captive breeding program. Thinking deeply about what mattered most to me, I decided to research the conservation of

Hawaiian birds and make a contribution to a project that would benefit the Palila or another endemic bird, perhaps the Alalā. Even so, I had to struggle with the decision.

As we were driving from one end of the Big Island to the other, making our move, Susan and I talked at more length about my erstwhile plans. I talked about the Palila and what had interested me about the species. But, I told her, I had decided to surrender the Palila. It really was not necessary that I see it. Susan then told me that she had reconsidered her plans as well and thought it would be okay for me to spend the time I had allocated to birding. Still concerned about the rental car policy, though, she asked if there was some other way I might see the bird without driving on Saddle Road. I thought not, but then, over lunch, I discovered that a tour company regularly takes birders into the area. I called them and they were going to Saddle Road the very next day. Unfortunately, they would depart early in the morning from Kona, a three-hour drive from our location south of Hilo. Once again, I surrendered the Palila.

Later in the afternoon, Susan realized she was tired and wanted to sleep in the next day, and then work on her book. "What do you think?" she asked. "Is it worth the risk, taking the car on Saddle Road?" After reflecting for a moment, I decided it was. The next morning I welcomed the dawn from lower Saddle Road. I made a few stops where I saw Apapane, I'iwi, Hawaii Amakihi, and other birds, but I was eager to get to Puu Laau. Saddle Road had been easy driving—entirely paved, with painted center and side stripes, and I couldn't see the basis for the rental company's concern. The gravel road at the Kilohana hunter's station was something else, again. Initially bumpy and deeply rutted, it made me wonder if I would have to either walk four miles in and four miles back, or surrender the Palila after all. But before I could find a place to even consider turning around, the road smoothed out and it was easy driving the rest of the way.

I drove along with the window rolled down, and I soon came into mamane forest. Nearly half an hour later, a few tenths of a mile short of the area where the bird is supposedly best seen, I stopped the car and turned off the engine. Was it intuition, or having heard an unfamiliar call out of awareness? I may never know. I got out, walked up a little hill to a cluster of mamane trees, and there among the bright yellow blossoms was a Palila! A chunky bird nearly the size of an Evening Grosbeak, gorgeous with a heavy dark bill, dark lores and short dark eyeline against a yellow hood, the Palila fanned his broad gray tail and showed yellow primaries contrasting with a dark gray back and pale gray belly, while singing a querulous whistled song. Moments later, another bird arrived, and I watched them for several minutes until they moved on. Later in the morning, there were good views of several other.

There were more endemics to be found at the Hawaii Volcanoes National Park, and other lifers elsewhere on the island in subsequent days. Susan and I drove around the island together. We went to the beach, dined out, and enjoyed some romantic afternoon time together. After I got back home, I sent a donation to a fund with active and successful programs for protecting native birds in Hawaii for the amount I would have paid for the guided tour. It seemed the least I could do for the Palila, after surrendering it only to find it after all.

My experience with the Palila left me with a new vision of myself: learning to surrender the things I've always wanted, while remaining open to receiving them anyway.

(August 5, 2002, Hilo, HI)

LIVING IN THE MOMENT

"Life can be found only in the present moment."
Thich Nhat Hahn, in *Present Moment, Wonderful Moment*

The present moment is all that is real. The past is gone, to be seen again only in karmic echoes; the future is imaginary. Given the truth of this premise, it is astonishingly difficult for most of us to situate ourselves firmly in the moment. As Pema Chödrön points out, a major impediment involves our stories. We tell stories about the past, about our birding triumphs, regrets, recriminations and failures. We tell stories about the future, about our hopes and dreams and fears. We tell stories to others (bragging, apologizing) and to ourselves (excuses, self-criticisms).

The sorts of stories we tell—whether to others or only ourselves—begin to organize themselves into themes or story lines that may take on the appearance of reality even though the thematic idea is quite unreal. It is only by learning to let go of our story lines that we are enabled to begin waking up and reconnecting with reality. This removes us from the security and comfort we find in our familiar illusions, and yet, as Chödrön explains, the unfamiliar terrain is where we can find liberation in the "healing water of bodhichitta". It is not that being in the present moment provides us with sanctuary or refuge, but rather that it gives access to the vast potential of flexibility and uncertainty. The only true story line is what is unfolding right now.

Birds exhibit unique capabilities in simultaneously being in the moment and being "on task." Migration begins on schedule and proceeds according to seasonal variables, and all along the route, birds are feeding and protecting themselves in the moment.

Sudden Rarities

Of course, birders can be as susceptible as anyone to living in the past or the future, instead of in the present. As just noted, Zen teaches that the future does not exist, except as the consequence of present action; nor is the past real, except as the karmic burden borne by the present. Thich Nhat Hahn points out that if given an abstract choice, we generally would choose life over death. Yet we often act in a contrary way, moving relentlessly in the direction of the future, the direction in which we will encounter death.

Birders express this contrary direction by excessive focus on listing or ticking. Spiritual growth can be found in transcending one's list.

How joyous to see a species of bird new to you! But this event always takes place in the present. To affirm life, it is important to truly see the bird, to see yourself in the same place and the same present moment of time with the bird, to experience yourself being with the bird. It is only in the present moment that we can fully experience a unique fellow creature as real. As soon as we surrender that moment, stepping away from the bird and ticking it off our list, we have let that beautiful creature slip back into the realm of abstractions. Also, we personally are then one tick closer to our final lifer.

How fruitless to resist that last lifer. We cannot forestall death by refusing to keep a list! But we can choose to find our primary joy, which can be shared with others, in being with the bird, rather than in checking it off our list. Also, an intention to live in the present moment can give us a new perspective about "dipped" species (birds we hoped to see but missed). The dipped bird can be understood like a red light when we are driving—in Thich Nhat Hahn's words, as "a bodhisattva helping us to return to the present moment." The dipped bird can be taken as a small lesson in self-discipline.

Perception of time, per se, is constant. Perception of time vis-à-vis our lives, i.e., ego-based time, is structured in terms of the percentage of our life represented by a given unit of time. At age ten, a year is ten percent of one's life—a big chunk. But at age fifty, a year is only two percent—a relatively tiny fraction. Thus time appears to move faster, the older one gets.

We never have "enough time," not even when we think we have enough time. There may be one exception. Big Listers who start young have more years in which to build their lists. Peter Kaestner is an example; he says "Time is my weapon."

In the Present

In the mid-1980s, I flew from California to a conference in Charleston, South Carolina. On Sunday, the day of my return, I got up very early and glanced hurriedly at my itinerary. My flight didn't leave until 7 p.m.!

I dashed off birding, and got my lifer American Oystercatcher at Folly Beach, sometime in mid-afternoon. Afterwards I raced to the airport, arriving just in time... in time, that is, to discover that 7 p.m. was when my plane arrived back in Los Angeles. The flight had left shortly before noon! I spent the night in the airport, trying to rebook a flight. But I got the bird!

(1983, Charleston, SC)

What is "enough time"? Differently put, we only have "enough time" when we *decide* we have enough time—only this generally cannot be a thinking decision. It can only be a *realization*, deeply felt, that whatever "amount" of time is allotted to us is sufficient for some larger purpose or in some larger context that we glimpse, but dimly, if at all.

The Moment

The remedy: live in and for the moment. I can do this in birding. My morning walk takes a bit more than an hour. It covers two to three miles. I see certain species of birds, and certain numbers of birds, depending on the time of day, the season, and the weather, but depending only minimally on myself in any ego-centered sense. What makes this walk a meditation is my one simple rule: I can see, hear, think whatever comes to me, but it must be in present tense— anything so long as it's not a review of yesterday or plans for tomorrow or later today. In this way, birding time (although we may nonetheless think it all too limited) is a constant.

Birds can help us locate ourselves in the moment, and they can assist in escaping from our conscious thoughts. After a few minutes of zazen at a session in Santa Fe, the roshi asked, "Where are you now?" He chuckled and said, "See how hard it is?" He was assuming that we were lost in thought. Instead, I was breathing with a Spotted Towhee, a Mourning Dove, and a Western Scrub Jay, all of them calling repeatedly outside.

(2002 Santa Fe, NM)

It is only in this present moment that we can patiently relish the possibility of seeing some long wanted particular bird, and it is only in the present moment that we may see something entirely unexpected. So it was when I found the fourth spring record of a Canada Warbler at the Oasis Ranch in Inyo County, California; and so it was when I found a singing male Baltimore Oriole at Marymoor Park.

(2006 Redmond, WA, near Seattle)

APPRECIATION OF PLACE

Birders' appreciation of place extends to places where non-birders are disinclined to spend time; these include cemeteries, dumps and sewage treatment facilities. The municipal dump at Brownsville TX is the only reliable place in the U.S. to see the Mexican Crow (*Corvus imparatus*). Sewage treatment plants, such as the Avra Valley Wastewater Treatment Plant west of Tucson AZ, attract waterfowl not easily found elsewhere in the vicinity. San Antonio's Mitchell Lake, a former wastewater lagoon now converted to a wildlife refuge with an Audubon Center, has the only shorebird-supporting mudflats in central Texas.

The pleasure in cemetery birding is, in part, the joy of finding diverse life in a place explicitly devoted to the remembrance of death, yet this is a relatively trivial metaphoric observation. There is also delight in finding an alternative personal use, truly celebratory, for places that most people approach either in mourning or with morbid curiosity. We may also reflect on the matter of land use. There are those, thoroughly imbued with a secular humanist point of view, who think of cemeteries as a waste of valuable urban space. Useful neither for commerce nor organized recreation (so goes the logic), what benefit accrues to society from this allocation of open land? Indeed. Except that where else, save in a cemetery, can one go in an urban environment to sit quietly under a tree, observe nature, and reflect on life and death?

Blue Jay perched on the gravestone of Frank Hennaman (Colonel, U.S. Army, 1895-1949) and his wife Martha (1893-1966). Would they have thought the jay a better decoration than flowers?

Northern Mockingbird perched atop a pyramidal monument to the Coast Guard Cutter Tampa, sunk by an enemy submarine with loss of all on board in September 1918.

Yellow-shafted Flicker on the tombstone of Henry Marshall Donehoo (Capt., 17th Pennsylvania Calvary, 1835-1899, and his wife Elizabeth McCreery—no dates of birth or death).

American Crow dramatically perched on a standard issue tombstone marked "UNKNOWN U.S. SOLDIER," cawing and giving surrogate voice to one who has been long silent.

Chipping Sparrow hopping around inside a fancy tombstone, roofed with miniature stone columns (John Andrew Wilcox, Colonel U.S. Calvary, 1828-1913).

Eastern Kingbird flycatching from a snag in a tree next to the John F. Kennedy gravesite. "Here on earth God's work must truly be our own." – JFK
   (1983, Arlington National Cemetery, VA)

Many cemeteries are renowned for their birding potential. Prominent among these are the Mount Auburn Cemetery (Cambridge MA), Old City Cemetery (Lynchburg VA), Spring Grove Cemetery (Cincinnati OH), Green Lawn Cemetery & Arboretum (Columbus OH) and Evergreen Cemetery (Portland ME). Two of our favorites have been the Wildwood Cemetery in Amherst MA, and the Fairview Cemetery in Santa Fe NM.

PRACTICING PATIENCE

If birding is anything, it is a practice of patience. According to Shunryu Suzuki, the Japanese word *nin*, usually translated as patience, can alternatively be translated as "constancy." Michael Harwood wrote about his father finally having seen a

Yellow-breasted Chat after fifty years of "patient waiting." The bird suddenly appeared to him, through a window, as he was buttoning his shirt.

Loss and Impatience

On Kauai, I met a birder couple from Texas. They were looking for Red-billed Tropicbird, but got impatient and left about 15 minutes before I found the bird. They had gone to the Big Island first. They saw the Palila with a Touring Company, and they did a second day with them as well. Here on Kauai, they are doing a charter pelagic trip with some British birders, and next they're going to Maui. The woman said, "We hired a guide. She told us she'd guarantee the parrot-bill and the other two—I forget what they are. You have to pay the Nature Conservancy, too, but I don't mind that. With a good guide you get transportation, they give you lunch, they take you in and point at the bird. It has its advantages."

(July 26, 2002, Kauai, HI)

A big advantage—perhaps paramount for these two—is that you get to tick the bird off your list! A big disadvantage is that you may not remember, the next day, what the bird was.

The Red-Billed Pigeon

Waiting for a much-desired bird can be a meditative experience. This was first made clear to me at the Santa Ana National Wildlife Refuge in Texas, in 1990. One of the birds I most wanted to see during that trip to the lower Rio Grande was a Red-billed Pigeon. My typical birding style at the time was one of near-constant movement. I would drive from place to place and walk the trails, but I would stop only to quickly look and listen for birds. At most, I would wait a minute or two, try briefly pishing for birds, and then if nothing appeared, I would move on. May 2ⁿᵈ found me exploring Santa Ana National Wildlife Refuge, but I "dipped" on the Red-billed Pigeon. That night, at Bentsen State Park, I met another birder, Jim, who had seen the Red-billed at Santa Ana. I decided to return the next day.

Back at Santa Ana, I had no sooner entered a roofed blind at the edge of a pond than it started raining. The rain began shortly after 7:30 a.m. and continued rather hard. During the first hour I was kept busy with other birds: a Ringed Kingfisher, a pair of Black-bellied Whistling Ducks, a flock of Long-billed Dowitchers, eight Tricolored Herons, a Common Moorhen, a Black-necked Stilt, and a Purple Gallinule. During the next hour, I saw Snowy Egrets, a Common Yellowthroat, a Great Kiskadee, and a Green Kingfisher. I heard Plain Chachalacas, but I was growing increasingly impatient. I thought about moving on, despite the rain, but where would I go?

I remembered Jim's Red-billed Pigeon at this location the previous day, and I convinced myself to settle down. During the third hour, I had Barn Swallows, Gadwalls, a White-tipped Dove, a Sora, a Groove-billed Ani and, best of all, a close-up view of a Least Grebe. By the time it quit raining, about 10:30 a.m., I was no longer fixated on my wristwatch. Without realizing it, I was in a miniature sesshin, *a silent meditative retreat. No additional species showed themselves, and it didn't matter in the least. I was quietly and calmly meditating on the Red-billed Pigeon—being somehow aware of Red-billed Pigeons without consciously thinking about them— when, a bit before 11 a.m., I heard a hoarse cooing with a very different rhythm from the call of the White-tipped Dove. I searched the treetops from which the sound was emanating, and there it was—my Red-billed Pigeon, more beautiful than I expected with his pale maroon throat and breast, and all the more appreciated because of the time I had spent waiting for him.*

(1990, Santa Ana National Wildlife Refuge, TX)

Brown-Capped Rosy-Finch

Doug, Walt and I had more or less conceded that the birds we initially saw in flight were probably crossbills instead of Rosy-Finches, and we decided to go into the restaurant for a cup of hot tea and an opportunity to warm up, as temperatures were quite frigid. We drove back to the upper parking lot, got out, and there in the conifers were dozens of Rosy-Finches!

We postponed the hot tea for 15 minutes or so, looking at the Rosy-Finches through Doug's scope, and at close range when they came to the snow bank on the north side of the parking lot.

Black Rosy-Finches were easily identified, along with smaller numbers of Gray-crowned Rosy-Finches—even a couple of Hepburn's. But the Brown-capped eluded us. We couldn't figure what, exactly, we were looking for.

Over tea, we studied the Sibley guide. A simplified head-color formula became apparent to me:

(1) Gray-crowned Rosy-Finch: gray head, brown body
(2) Black Rosy-Finch: black cap on gray body, dark gray-black body
(3) Brown-capped Rosy-Finch: entirely gray—little or no head/body contrast

Back outside, we soon had the Brown-capped as well. We also noted that we have very compatible styles of birding. We're intensely interested, willing to stand around in the cold waiting to see a bird we want, but also willing to take a break and have a cup of tea. Sometimes, easing off like that is more productive than unrelenting effort.

(January. 20, 2003, Santa Fe, NM)

Capulin Spring

Last week I was at Capulin Spring late in the afternoon. Today, I arrived before dawn. I was not there simply to look, listen and discover what could be seen and heard. I went because other birders had reported Northern Saw-whet Owls. These are tiny owls, smaller than a robin. I've never seen or heard one. There are also Flammulated Owls in the area, and although I've heard them calling before, I've never seen one.

Arriving at 5:30 a.m., I had seen and heard more than a dozen species of birds by seven, but no owls.

I found myself meditating on the concept of patience.

"Have patience," an inner voice told me, "and a Saw-whet will appear, right before your eyes." But no owls came. (True, the voice had not said when.)

"Patience is not about quietly waiting," the voice said. "Patience is being unaware of waiting." Still, no owls came.

All morning, there had been birds at the spring—but two or three birds, only, and never more than two species at once. Suddenly, there was a flush of activity. There were Hermit Thrushes and Robins, Steller's Jays, a Hairy Woodpecker and a Red-shafted Flicker, Yellow-rumped and Virginia's Warblers, Pine Siskins and Red-breasted Nuthatches, all at once. I was enthralled.

When things calmed down, I realized that for a few minutes, I had been patient, and I realized that while patience doesn't necessarily produce the birds we're seeking, it does allow us to live outside of the waiting.

(2003, Capulin Spring, NM)

Observing the patience of birds can be instructive.

An adult male Ladder-backed Woodpecker is feeding a youngster, patiently taking bite after bite of suet and passing it to the big baby. The young bird accepts bite after bite, but then there's a shuffling retreat back down the branch when the parent brings the next morsel.

What is going on? I look more closely and chuckle to see that the juvenile bird has a glob of suet stuck on the tip of his upper mandible *and cannot get it off. There's a bit of experimentation, and finally, finally, the little woodpecker manages to wipe the suet onto a branch, and then eat it. The parent waited while this took place, and then continued the feeding.*

I laughed, and then I wondered. Am I as patient as this woodpecker father when I'm trying to give something to someone who's not ready for it? Is there anything in my life that's right on the tip of my nose, but nonetheless a bit beyond my grasp?

(June 13th, 2005, Santa Fe NM)

Some would think that doing a bird census while taking a morning walk is obsessive. Rather, it can be a disciplined way of staying in the moment. It is possible to be at one's Zen best when on a familiar path with familiar birds – here, now, and open to finding the unexpected.

Chapter 5

TRANSCENDENT BEAUTY
IN THE MUNDANE

"Nature is reality, and worthy of awe in the perceptions of the person who practices a culturally conditioned "tuning in" of the natural world. He or she sees, hears, smells and tastes the natural world with greater acuity. The body feels the subtle forces of nature with greater acuity."
– Gregory Cajete, *Native Science.*

While doing walking meditation in Santa Fe, we proceeded down an arroyo, then back up the road – sensing the earth and its attendant beings breathing. Trees breathe out clouds. Chamisa bushes breathe in water vapor and use it to break apart rocks with its roots.

Meditation can bring us to unexpected beauty and insight. Try experiencing the hardnesses and softnesses of your body and of the earth, and feel how breath creates hardness from softness, and softness from hardness.

Be attentive to watchers of birds who are neither birdwatchers nor birders. These are people for whom birds are simply a part of their world, to be noticed because of their beauty, skills or habits.

Standing in a parking lot with Tribal Council members at Picuris Pueblo, in northern New Mexico, one man gestured toward an Osprey flying over the tribal fishing lake. "There goes the fisherman," he said. "He'll get a fish, and then he'll take it to that cottonwood right over there, and he'll eat it." We stood talking a few moments longer, and sure enough, it happened just as he had predicted. No one was surprised.

Then too, unexpected beauty may stalk us, without any effort on our part to seek it out.

The Unexpected

At 5 degrees F., this was the coldest morning of the year in Santa Fe, and when I started from the house to the studio shortly after 7 a.m., I noticed that Western Scrub-Jays were raising a ruckus down slope from the house. It wasn't just the jays. There were four Canyon Towhees, two Spotted Towhees, a half-dozen House Finches, a half-dozen Dark-eyed Juncos (Pink-sided and Oregon) and two Northern (Red-shafted) Flickers, all gathered around a small thicket of young junipers. All were active and vocal, as were American Robins in the big willow tree near the house.

Soon enough I found the target of group ire—a Great Horned Owl, on the ground, apparently just having been driven from the juniper thicket. The owl waddled toward me, blinking and looking befuddled. The amazing thing was that he was covered with frost and sparkling in the early morning sunlight!

Then the owl took flight, and the whole mob of juncos and finches, towhees and jays, took off right after him. The robins flew en masse from the willow, 32 of them in all, and they chased the owl over to the house next door, where the owl perched briefly before going off to find another hiding place.

(February 13, 2005, Santa Fe NM)

Beauty is to be heard as well as seen.

Listening to the dawn chorus this morning, I resisted the urge to begin listing all the species I could hear. It is, of course, inter-

esting — and potentially important — to know who is out there, but too intent a focus on this can detract from a musical experience. Instead of picking out a dozen different voices, I simply let myself be immersed in the rich sounds of an ecosystem singing.

(May 22, 2005, Santa Fe NM)

Finding beauty is not always easy. We sometimes must look closely, and we must look with attitude as well as with eyes.

"Shit!" someone might say, in an exclamation of disgust. "Whitewash!" a birder exclaims in eager anticipation, pointing out pale streaks on a cliff face or in a tree — readily visible evidence of a perch frequently used by a hawk or owl, who may be nearby.

Excrement is excrement, but our attitude about it hinges on our awareness. Nothing in nature is useless, even though we may be blind to its value.

Gratitude

A few years ago, in Aroostook County, Maine, I spent the morning paddling a canoe from one side of Cross Lake to the other seeing birds, moose, and deer. I felt nothing but gratitude that we still have places such as this, as wild as this and even wilder. I could have focused on the fact that the west side of the lake had been logged repeatedly and that the virgin forest is long gone. I could have resented the string of "camps" (vacation homes) that dot the eastern shore of the lake. But gratitude is necessary if we're to make the effort for conservation and preservation of the earth.

(August 2, 2002, Caribou, ME)

Hand in hand with gratitude must go forgiveness. There were those who argued, before the captive breeding program was begun for the California Condor, that the species should be allowed to go extinct "and then the world will see." A deep vindictiveness underlay that attitude. It is quite unclear what "the world" has seen about extinction of the Dodo, the Carolina Parakeet, and the Passenger Pigeon. To preserve the world and its marvelous inhabitants, we need to forgive human short-sightedness and work tirelessly toward educating others about what remains possible.

Junk Birds

Some birders talk about introduced species as "trash birds" or "junk birds." Perhaps the widespread North American disapprobation of European Starlings and House Sparrows is justified. House Sparrows pugnaciously evict bluebirds and swallows from their nest cavities, and Starlings are determined cavity nesters who have adapted to an astonishing variety of ecological niches, displacing many native species of less aggressive temperament.

People with disparaging views of these birds tend to be devoted environmentalists, and people who love them often are quite unaware of environmental issues. But it is not that simple. First off, it is important to know that European birders see the situation quite differently. House Sparrows and European Starlings are natives in Europe, and although much beloved by many, their populations have diminished in recent years. European birders are distressed, and they are seeking solutions to the problem. Beyond that, it is important that we ask ourselves precisely what disturbs us about these birds in our own back yards.

Two things seem to provoke birders into using the epithet "trash bird." One is the mere fact of being common, while the other has to do with a bird's willingness to associate with our own species. Some folks will dismiss almost any sort of bird as "trash." For instance, after seeing a half dozen Scarlet Tanagers during a walk through the woods, someone might exclaim, "They're trash birds, here!" Such comments are usually made in jest. Even so, does this suggest that birds are considered mere collectibles, and valuable only if scarce?

Chimango Caracaras are a "trash bird" of the Argentine countryside, and they're common in urban environments as well. There is an Argentine idiom for urging people not to squander efforts or resources: "Don't waste gunpowder on Chimangos."

But when American birders extend their loathing to House Finches, even in western states where they are native—merely because these little birds are quite comfortable living in close proximity to humans—one may begin to wonder. Do we hate these birds simply for who and what they are, or is this displaced self-loathing?

It is true that members of the "trash bird triumvirate" (as I've heard Rock Pigeons, House Sparrows and European Starlings called) are comfortable in the most boring of suburbs, as well as the most sterile urban settings. But is this the fault of the birds?

A few considerations: First, we must clean our own nests, and improve those unconscious habits of ours that continue to spoil human habitats. Second, we must become aware of our foolish expansion into every available niche on the planet. We need to realize the rights of other beings, in sharing the riches of this planet. And third, we need to become conscious that this wealth may cease to exist if the only remaining life on earth is human and whatever else we are able to engineer and manipulate.

As for "trash birds", so long as other living creatures can adapt to our suburbs and cities, on their own terms, not ours, this is reason for hope rather than despair. This does not mean that we must look the other way when House Sparrows attack Bluebirds in the nest boxes we've put out. Intervention, when our modifications of the environment have put native species at risk, is entirely reasonable. But there are places where "trash birds" are the only ones that can adapt, and so long as this is the case, we should be grateful for them. We must be attentive to circumstances in which introduced species are less harmful than we expected.

Circumstances

At the Fairview Cemetery, there are Lewis's Woodpeckers, apparently nesting in cavities in the big hackberry trees. This small urban forest is heavily populated by European Starlings, but Lewis's Woodpeckers are one species able to resist the non-native birds. Introduced species do indeed cause many problems, but natives may be more resilient than we sometimes think.

(July 6, 2005, Santa Fe NM)

Watching Starlings In Albuquerque

European Starlings are the birds that North American birders most intensely love to hate. They disdain House Sparrows and Rock Pigeons, but they almost universally despise starlings. Yet on many occasions one hears a birder ruefully remark, "You know, if it weren't a starling, it'd be beautiful."

There are, of course, objective reasons for disliking starlings. From a few pairs released in Central Park during the nineteenth century as part of a Shakespearean festival (the species is mentioned in Henry IV Part 1), the starling population has exploded across North America. More opportunist than generalist, starlings now occupy an amazing range of niches. Starlings can be found in cities, suburbs, farms, woodland, and beaches. Here an urban scavenger; there a usurper of woodpecker holes in cottonwood bosques and saguaro forests; and there again poking through wracks of seaweed, side-by-side with Black and Ruddy Turnstones.

Late this afternoon, standing outside a shoe store along Montgomery Avenue in Albuquerque, I found myself watching starlings. About a dozen of them were perched on a high-strung utility line overlooking the shopping center. They made occasional forays down to the parking lot, or onto rooftops or into alleys behind the stores, but mostly they occupied themselves by socializing with each other.

There was much fidgeting, sometimes solitary. One bird would raise a wing and turn its head as if sniffing its wingpit. Another would shrug both wings two or three times. Still another would suddenly shudder as if contemplating something horrific. But most often, the fidgeting was social. A bird would take flight, wheel around and land just on the opposite side of its neighbor. Sometimes the landing bird would nonchalantly look the opposite direction from the neighbor, but on other occasions both birds would hop and turn to look in the same direction. By far the favorite move was a series of rapid sidesteps, a transparent attempt—almost always successful—to provoke the neighbor into edging farther away.

We all know that starlings are intensely social. They congregate in flocks of hundreds of thousands, and their coordinated flight, wheeling and twisting and turning, is pure visual poetry. But how often do we stop to notice the interactions among a handful of them? They can be fascinating to watch, and comical as well. Watching them, I realized that in more ways than one, they remind me of people.

(November 13, 2000; Albuquerque NM)

Sentient Beings

It is a particularly human conceit to think we are the only sentient beings. Observation tells us that other animals have no such illusions. Lions and wildebeests, kestrels and buntings, recognize one another as predator and prey, and each knows the other has the ability to capture or to elude. Insisting that we are sentient, and all others are dumb, is clinging to an arbitrarily narrow perspective that allows us to do great violence to others—and ultimately, to ourselves as well.

Children seem to intuitively grasp the kinship among humans, birds, and other animals. It is our challenge as adults to learn from them, and to help children remember these things they know so well. A favorite story of ours involves a friend and her then five-year-old son. She parked her car under a tree in the driveway one night, and the next morning swore at the birds for pooping on her windshield. "But Mom," protested the son, "They don't have anyplace else to go!"

A Cat With Buddha Nature

My brother has a cat, Stella, who has Buddha nature, and with it, she has given up chasing birds. Stella's enlightenment requires practice. Rick and Kristina hold Stella in their laps as they chant Nichiren Daishonin's Nam-myoho-renge-kyo, daily. If they skip a couple of days, Stella regresses, but so long as they chant with her, there is peaceful coexistence with birds. Stella still has growth possibilities. Although she is able to calmly regard even some brash and colorful birds, such as male Northern Cardinals, Mourning Doves invariably agitate her. Even so, she doesn't chase them. "We can't decide, Rick says, whether she's a Kittysatva or a Bodhikitva."

(December 23, 2001, Pensacola, FL)

A Zen story tells of a neophyte who asked his roshi (teacher) if his dog had Buddha nature. "Yes," replied the roshi, "but he's done very little with it."

Sidney's Purple Martin

One spring day in 1953, my friend Sidney Smith brought a Purple Martin in a shoebox for third-grade show-and-tell. He said he had found the bird with a broken wing and had nursed it back to health. My classmates crowded around to look at the bird and were delighted and intensely interested in everything Sidney was telling them.

Personally, the sight of the poor bird crouching in the corner of the tiny box, obviously in mortal fear, horrified me. I urged Sidney to let the bird loose; it was well now, wasn't it?

Yes, it was, but Sidney was unmoved by my pleas. He was going to keep the bird forever—and, I imagined, forever in a tiny shoebox. I myself kept animals caged—snakes, lizards and turtles, but not birds. On occasions when I found injured birds, I kept them only until they were well.

Sadly, I formulated a plan. I always walked home for lunch while the other students ate in the school cafeteria. On this day, I went home, gobbled my lunch and hurried back to school. Arriving before the teacher and my classmates returned, I rushed into the cloakroom and brought out the shoebox prison. I went to an open window.

I debated with myself. Either way, I knew there would be a loss. There would be Sidney's anger to deal with, not to mention that of the other children and the teacher. I almost put the bird back, but I looked at it again and noticed that, despite the holes Sidney had punched in the box, the martin seemed to be having difficulty breathing.

The choice was finally clear. It was a life versus friendship, a life versus social acceptance and understanding. The decision was also clear. Although the life was only that of a young Purple Martin, I had to save the life.

Taking a deep breath, slyly for the bird as well as for myself, I lifted the bird from the box and placed him on the windowsill. Even as the bird took wing, I felt my spirit soaring in exhilaration, yet simultaneously, even as I dropped the shoebox on the floor, I felt a crushing weight of guilt.

Nothing else that happened that day remains in my memory, nothing specific. I do not know how my deed was discovered. Perhaps I announced it. More likely, I denied it even though I would clearly have been the only suspect. I do know that my guilt was eventually established, and everyone—Sidney, my classmates, the teacher—was angry with me.

I do not know whether I was stubborn and defensive, or deeply repentant. I do know that Sidney and I were never friends after that day. I also know that, although I felt pangs of guilt in regard to the incident for several years thereafter, there was always the additional feeling that regardless of consequences there was no other authentic option available.

Many years later, I released a bird that had been trapped inside a house. As he shot into the sky, my spirit soared with him and for one brief moment I was once again the child of twenty-some years before, but this time, with conscious, unfettered pride.

(July 17, 2002, Santa Fe, NM)

A primary vow in Buddhism is to save all beings. If that status is extended to birds, the importance of conservation is brought to the fore.

Conservation is not a desperate, defensive effort. It is, instead, joyous and life-affirming. Many campaigns have been remarkably successful. The National Audubon Society was organized around an effort to halt the slaughter of Great Egrets and Snowy Egrets for their feathers, used for fashionable women's hats. Absent this campaign, egrets may have gone extinct. Instead, their populations are healthy and expanding.

Furthermore, conservation is something that can be profoundly affected at the local, even backyard—level. A key need for North American birds is freedom from roaming cats. Cats are very good at flushing little animals out from under cover, and where there are lots of cats, there are very few quails or other ground-dwelling birds. Some people point out that it's natural for cats to hunt, and from the standpoint of their biology, it is. What's not natural about house cats going out and hunting is that people are feeding them every day, so the cats don't have to compete in a natural way by preying on quail and other birds. If they did, there would be very few house cats around, because an area could only sustain so many of them. It's a matter of balance. Nature provides balance, but unconscious human behavior doesn't. When every third or fourth house has a subsidized cat that runs loose, many wild birds perish—particularly ground-nesting birds.

Patience and Conservation

During the past year, we've acquired new neighbors with an outdoor cat, and quail have been scarce ever since. One of my worries was relieved when, during my morning walk on the greenbelt, I spied distant movement around a grove of junipers. Scanning with my binoculars, I saw a pair of Scaled Quails, and then I counted ten tiny chicks scurrying through the grasses with their parents. They will of course face many obstacles between now and the time that they, in turn, might become parents, but every species is perpetuated one brood at a time.

(August 9, 2005, Santa Fe NM)

From perhaps fifteen thousand birds at the time of first European arrival in North America, Whooping Cranes—

frequently shot for food, or to prevent them from eating grain—declined to a mere thirteen birds in 1941. After Robert Porter Allen's 1946 discovery of the last breeding area, in Saskatchewan's Wood Buffalo National Park, after establishment of a U.S. Fish and Wildlife Service recovery program in 1967, and after designation of the species as Endangered in 1970, the population gradually and slowly increased. Most of the birds are part of a migratory flock that winters at Aransas National Wildlife Refuge in Texas. Despite the failed attempt to establish a second migratory flock at the Bosque del Apache NWR and setbacks with non-migratory flocks, the species is on the rebound. Two hundred and thirty-six birds migrated back north from Aransas in the spring of 2007. There are now small non-migratory flocks at Barabou, Wisconsin, and on the Kissimmee Prairie in Florida. Along with captive populations at the Patuxent Wildlife Research Center in Maryland and a half-dozen plus zoos in the U.S. and Canada, there were 453 Whooping Cranes as of March 2005.

As Wendell Berry (*Life is a Miracle: An Essay Against Modern Superstition*) has so cogently argued, life is a miracle. Look around you. Miracles, large and small, are everywhere. Life itself is a miracle, and so is our capability to perpetuate the diversity of life on our planet. But this does not mean that we can expect life to do absurd things. We must become aware of diversity and what is needed to support it, and we must take the appropriate actions.

It is of utmost importance to understand that successful conservation efforts do not start with intellectual understanding. They start with opening of the heart. "Crocodile Hunter" Steve Irwin often expressed that humans want to save what they love.

There is, among "serious" birders, a tendency to idealize nature. They set themselves the task of finding nature unspoiled by human hands. But, sadly for those who allow themselves such melancholy, nature unspoiled is now at least a few centuries in the past, as shown by Bill McKibben in *The End of Nature*. Instead of seeking "unspoiled" nature, we would do better to recognize and facilitate multipurpose open space.

Openings for Conservation

John Heinz National Wildlife Refuge did not make an initial good impression. A crucial sign at a turn was hidden by roadside shrubbery. Waterways were strewn with trash (largely a result of recent floods). Urban noise—freeway traffic, sirens and airplanes—was a constant intrusion. The air was the same smoggy miasma that chokes the city elsewhere. To top it off, a feral feline wandered around by the Visitor Center.

But I chatted briefly with a tough-looking tattooed young man, and his face brightened as he told me what a wonderful place the refuge is: "It goes on and on!" And indeed, for all its downsides, it is undoubtedly the biggest open space in or near the city.

(October 4, 2004, John Heinz NWR, Philadelphia PA)

"Feeder birders" participate in their own sort of unreality. Some—not all—of these good people attempt to impose their own morality on the birds they feed. They overlook the realities of food chains, for instance, by criticizing accipiters who take advantage of goldfinches or siskins crowding around feeders.

Imposing our morality on birds is but a remnant of a once rampant way of thinking, in which all birds and animals were classified by their "economic value" to mankind. This was, in fact, useful insofar as it helped many people realize that hawks are not pure villains.

A sense of kinship involves awareness of the needs of our kin and a willingness to make appropriate sacrifices for them. If my birding plans are inconvenienced by rain, I strive to remember the importance of rain in nourishing the earth and all the multitudes of beings that depend on the earth for their lives.

Kinship

Late in the afternoon, I drove into the mountains for a bit of birding but, once there, found that the trails in the National Forest had been closed due to extreme fire danger.

For a few moments, I felt unhappy about being excluded from the forest. Then, I began thinking not about myself and my ego-centered interest in making a little list of birds seen today. Instead, I began thinking about the birds, secure for the moment in areas protected not only from fire but also from noisy people, dogs and mountain bikes.

We should often ask ourselves, is it more important that we see birds, or that there be birds?

(June 23, 2005, Santa Fe NM)

At depth, spirituality is about relationship and intelligence. But intelligence involves far more than the peculiar sort of rationality that has evolved among human beings. Intelligence is about patterning, about the creation of relationships among various beings in the cosmos. How can it be that Fibonacci numbers characterize patterns as diverse as the arrangement of stars in the arms of spiral galaxies, or sunflower seeds on a floral head, or the whorls of a snail's shell? Intelligence does not come from a source external to the world. It is instead inherent in the world, soaked and satiated throughout every aspect of cosmic existence. Consider fractal patterns: seen in lightning bolts, in erosional patterns, in mineral dendrites, and in fern leaves.

Thinking and Awareness

Thinking about birds, and being aware of birds, are two different things. To develop a sense of kinship requires non-thinking awareness. Birding away from home requires conscious thought. Birding in a familiar place, with familiar birds, is mindful in a very different manner. The lilting flight of a Townsend's Solitaire distinguishes it from an American Robin in a way that I sense with my whole body. I feel it in my arms and shoulders. I can spot a Western Scrub-Jay a few hundred meters away, and with the first bobbling movement the jay makes I know, in my spine, who I'm seeing. I can, of course, verbalize what it is that I'm sensing in making such identifications. But to do so involves a different mode of knowing — the mode of conscious thought.

(June 2, 2005, Santa Fe, NM)

GROUNDING ONESELF IN EVERYDAY LIFE

Becoming aware of birds is an integral part of becoming aware of the world around us. In our increasingly "virtual" world, we progressively lose awareness of geography and of seasonality. Richard Louv in *Last Child in the Woods*, discusses "Nature Deficit Disorder" as an increasing disconnect from nature that contributes to childhood depression, obesity, and attention deficit disorder.

Ennui or world-weariness may be what leads some people to see obsession in other people's passions. One danger in spirituality occurs when people disdain the world because of its impermanence. Grounding oneself in the present moment is essential, for the present moment is all there really is in life. The sense of present moment after present moment helps us to understand impermanence. Passion for life can only come through grounding and this understanding of impermanence.

Grounding oneself is most easily accomplished if done for other than ego-centric reasons, or at least if not done with conscious ego-centered motives. Yet it is worth noting that contact with nature brings health benefits. Beth Baker, in "Rx Nature," (*Nature Conservancy Magazine* 2002) wrote that Howard Framkin, an environmental health professor at Emory University, reviewed 20 years of medical literature and published results in *The American Journal of Preventive Medicine* (2001). He found that "contact with other living organisms and with wilderness can reduce stress and improve well-being." Similarly, the *Cancer Nursing Journal* reported improved attention span and quicker return to "normality" among breast cancer patients who spent 20-30 minutes 3 times per week in "restorative activity, such as bird-watching."

Grounding oneself also involves being present in one's significant relationships. There are "birding widows" as well as "golf widows", and one's game is not improved when it takes place at the expense of quality human contact. Intensive birding efforts are especially challenging. David Simpson, in his introduction to the 2001 ABA Big Day Report, commented, "How two married guys can pull off a Big Year is beyond me. I was about ready to divorce myself after my attempts."

Being present in relationship with birds can be more difficult to imagine. This begins, of course, with doing no harm: respecting habitat, avoiding any sort of harassment, being judicious in pishing, photography, and use of tape recordings. On a positive note, we can provide for birds' needs with bird-friendly landscaping that includes food, water and shelter. Avoiding pesticide and herbicide use by eating organic foods decreases poison in habitats.

Beyond these practicalities, it is possible to devise rituals of recognition and gratitude. Roger Tory Peterson in *All Things Reconsidered: My Birding Adventures* tells how, during the early years of the Audubon Camp at Hog Island, Maine, Allan Cruickshank celebrated a personal ritual. "Whenever a new bird for the camp list was sighted on a boat trip into the bay, he would stand on his head on the fo'c'sle, until his wife, Helen, made him stop the practice."

A common Zen ritual, the *gassho*, is a formal greeting in which the palms of the hands are brought together in front of the chest and a slight bow is made. The gesture is made simply as a greeting and to express humility, respect, reverence and gratitude. Doing *gassho* for a new species on one's list, or for an "old friend" well seen, could become a meaningful personal observance to reinforce our perception of birds as beings with whom we can have significant relationships.

Birding and non-birding spouses can work together to create a sense of balance in their life. Remind a non-birding spouse that going out in nature together is an opportunity for improving physical fitness in pleasant surroundings, and she in turn, may remind you to also look at flowers and butterflies, not just birds.

Being spiritually grounded in our relationships means seeking out what works and devoting our energies toward enhancing those things. A wise family elder once remarked, after having lost her husband, "I realized I could either grieve, or celebrate what we had together." She recognized that our emotional energy is finite and that we must choose how we expend it. We can either focus on the negative, or on the positive.

Life is a series of choices. In certain ways that some birders would find peculiar, it is possible to be thankful when a spouse is a non-birder. Adjusting to his or her apparent disinterest in birds can facilitate one's own spiritual growth. Different perspectives often remind each of us that there is more to the world than we presently understand.

Inhale his point of view, exhale your own. Negotiation with a significant other is like *Zazen*. Being in a relationship is like breathing. Each moment depends on the moment before, and creates the moment next. Inhale, exhale, inhale; your view, mine, yours.

Many birders seem to enjoy whining about their non-birding spouses. There are, of course, challenges to be faced with non-birding spouses. They may not want to take a vacation in the same places we would choose, and even when they do, they could prefer lounging around on a relatively birdless beach rather than hiking into a birdy, but buggy, jungle.

Relationships change. Today's sense of balance, whether easily or hard-won, catches a wind and blows off in some other direction. Adjustments are eventually necessary even with a similarly obsessive birding spouse, and for the unprepared, this might be even more unsettling. Then, too, such shifts are required even if one is entirely on one's own. Retirement may mean moving into a smaller house or apartment. Even with ample financial resources, travel may become increasingly difficult with advancing age-related infirmities. Our hearing may fade. Our eyesight may fail.

Any of these circumstances may be the cause of suffering for the dedicated birder. For the Zen birder, though, these situations provide opportunities for greater understanding and acceptance of inevitable limits.

Balance is the key. See what you gain through what you give up; what you give in place of what you lose—*Zazen* again. If we only inhaled, without ever exhaling, we would burst; if we only exhaled, without ever inhaling, we would die.

Balance to Life

Recently, the news was dominated by stories of war and human violence. Everywhere—newspapers, radio, television—contained disquieting messages. That night, I dreamed about birds. They were doing nothing remarkable, of species that I expected to see in the coming weeks. There were warblers, and orioles, and black-headed grosbeaks hopping around in the shrubbery, feeding, singing. Nothing they were doing had any direct connection to human purposes, fears or aspirations. But this was precisely why the dream was so deeply reassuring. The earth still spins, leans on her axis, and revolves around the sun. Seasons still come and go. And this matters more to spirit and eternity than all the human dreams of empire and fears of insecurity.

(February 2006, Seattle, WA)

BEING PURPOSEFUL

To give up birding, while we are still able to draw a breath, can be immensely more difficult to accept. Celebrate the wind while we have it.

Hanging On: A Bewick's Wren

One blustery spring afternoon during my daily walk in Santa Fe, I watched with mild amazement as a little male Bewick's Wren clung to a dead snag atop a juniper tree—steadfastly hanging on despite a sustained breeze in excess of 20 miles per hour, and gusts that surely approached 30 mph.

Earlier in the day, a male Bewick's had been delivering a bubbly invitation for a mate from atop the apple tree next to our patio, and other males were doing the same from prominent perches in their intended territories all around the neighborhood. But the one I was watching in our tree near dusk was not singing. It was all he could do to simply hang on, leaning into the wind and taking aerodynamic advantage of his sharp little bill and sloped forehead, with wings pressed tightly against his body and his long tail involuntarily wagging behind him like a weathervane.

When I think of birds and wind, I am most inclined to think of birds on the wing, riding the wind in one way or another. Pelicans engage in "slope soaring"—gliding on a cushion of air in advance of a water wave. Hawks climb into the sky on thermals, barely moving a feather. They lean into a stiff breeze and bank their wings so that they stall and hang in midair—yes, like "kites." Gulls will tack into the wind, and then suddenly turn and let the current carry them swiftly in the other direction—"dynamic soaring".

It is instructive to note how birds go with the wind, even when they must go into it, and this of course is what we all must learn to do in life. But there are times in the lives of birds when the wind cannot be used to advantage. It must simply be endured.

I watched for several minutes as the Bewick's Wren resolutely gripped his chosen perch, apparently determined to wait until the wind relented enough for him to deliver another song or two before dark. But I moved on before the wren did, so I do not know who persisted longest — the wren or the wind.

Extremes of heat, cold, rain, and biting insects are discomforts that birders willingly endure. Wind can be another. Aside from a heavy pouring rain, wind is probably the most difficult condition for me to tolerate while birding. I can prepare for heat, cold, or moderate rainfall. I can take measures to minimize insect bites. But in a strong wind it is all I can do to simply hang on. Many birds — unlike the stubborn little Bewick's Wren — take refuge in leafy thickets during a windstorm, and even a gentle breeze obscures the movement of birds in a tree, making them difficult to see or hear. Nothing provokes me to "call it a day" more than a breeze that puts ten million cottonwood leaves into motion, each one rustling and trembling like a bird. I can only hang on, and hope the breeze will abate.

Eventually, of course, the wren gave up. He may have gotten in another song, or more; he may even have attracted a mate. But whether because of the steadfast wind or the dark, he finally "called it a day" and quit trying to sing. He was probably singing again the next morning, but perhaps not. For every wren, for every creature on this earth, there comes a season, a day, a moment, when we sing our last song.

(April 2, 2003, Santa Fe, NM)

Every birder must also, eventually, give it up. We must surrender life. We can recognize and accept that ultimate reality, as we recognize that the individual life is but half of a breath. We inhale the world, and we die and create the next moment of the world as we exhale.

Compromises, Acceptance Of Limits
The way out of suffering is the way into selfless, purposeful reconnection with the universe.

Patience and Capacity

Some condominiums and apartment buildings prohibit feeding birds due to the fear of birdseed attracting rodents. Yet others do not, and I have seen bird feeders outside of windows at assisted living facilities.

There are opportunities for seeing birds, and appreciating them, regardless of our circumstances. I once patronized a dentist who had a skylight directly over the dental chair. During several years of having my teeth cleaned, that small window afforded me fleeting views of nearly a dozen species of birds flying overhead.

(May 27, 2002, Santa Fe, NM)

Birding With Diminished Capacity

No matter what spiritual practice we undertake, if any, there will be times when the practice is relatively easy and times when it poses exceptional difficulty. The latter situations provide us with the greatest opportunity for awakening and grounding ourselves in reality. In Buddhist tradition, the fundamental love and goodness of all beings is known as *bodhichitta*. It is found on the warrior bodhisattva path where the enemies are self-deception and reactivity.

For birders who have long honed their skills in finding and identifying birds, the challenge becomes extreme when we find ourselves physically or mentally incapable of carrying out our usual activities. But whereas many opportunities vanish with diminished capacities, others open themselves in greater depth.

Diminished capacity can come upon us so gradually that we barely notice it, or it can pounce with sudden severity. Phoebe Snetsinger found it a gradual process, with diminishing stamina, and occasional pains becoming chronic. She roughly measured her physical decline by an increasingly high "peril-to-bird ratio."

Capacity and Patience

Relatively minor adjustments—on our own or with our birding companions—may be amusing, or even instructive. In California, I sometimes led an extra fieldtrip (in addition to the regular monthly Los Angeles Audubon trip) for a Sierra Club disabled group. I was initially impatient with the late start, the unloading of wheelchairs and motorized scooters, and the slow personal preparations. The crowd making the circuit around the big lake at Whittier Narrows was sometimes reminiscent of L.A.'s freeways. But I eventually relaxed. Group members were generally more observant and thoughtful than the usual crowd, and we often had better trip lists than on the regular trips, just because of our slow pace and the extra effort we made to be certain everyone had a decent look at all the birds.

Another example: My birding buddy Walt and I were driving the just-opened seasonal road at the Bosque del Apache National Wildlife Refuge near Socorro, New Mexico, when I heard a persistent chirping. I slowed the car to a crawl, and we slowly drove along an irrigation ditch and scanned the row of cottonwoods on its south side. I stopped periodically, consistently hearing the bird (which oddly kept pace with the car). Neither of us saw a potential culprit, and Walt didn't hear it. Several minutes passed before we realized that Walt had turned up the gain on his hearing aid, and this is what I'd been hearing. We enjoyed a good laugh, and then a good bird – a Common Black-Hawk rather well hidden in a cottonwood. We would likely have missed this one had we not been creeping along looking for the faux bird.

Whether gradually or quickly, many of us will find ourselves eventually challenged by unfamiliar realities that look and feel vastly different from our familiar and comfortable illusions of competence. Either way, we are confronted with a choice. We can slip back into ego-centered illusion, pitying ourselves for what we can no longer do well, or we can continue to work within the boundaries of remaining capacities and take the opportunity to develop our compassion for others who are facing similar constraints on their activities.

To simply give up on birding, in the face of diminished capacity—to withdraw from the fellowship with birds and birders—can be dangerous. Dan Koeppel wrote that "An all-consuming pursuit, by nature, leaves nothing in its wake, and when it ends, it can become a nearly annihilating force." This may be particularly true for the Zen birder, whose birding is an essential centering spiritual practice.

Some birders have come up with innovative solutions to their new limitations. At the simplest level, birders who are no longer capable of driving may extend their outings by teaming with younger or more capable birding buddies. Depending on the problem, new eyeglasses, a hearing aid, or memory-enhancing supplements may be helpful—or, more ambitious measures may be appropriate.

Mark Obmascik (*The Big Year*) relates the story of Leroy Jenson who, reaching his eighties and being no longer physically able to chase birds, did a worldwide Big Year from his television set in California. He watched and taped 1,800 shows, identifying a total of 1,136 species.

These imaginative innovations are testimony to the power of birds to organize our energies, although, in and of themselves, they would seem to primarily serve as ways of perpetuating accomplishment-oriented, ego-centered, approaches to birding. Diminished capacity offers opportunity to transcend ego focus; we can perhaps do this, and more.

Attempting to maintain or regain fading competency expresses the clichéd western dictum, *Carpe diem*! Seize the day. Go for it now; make the most of it; get it while the getting is good! A better and more realistic approach may be to recognize that although we can grasp at the day, it cannot be possessed.

We can of course inhabit the moment (in fact we must—it is our only option), but this gives no guarantee of a perfect trade-off. Our moments are our moments, and we cannot know whether they will be better or worse than those that follow. The challenge is simply—and profoundly—to make the best we can of each moment as it presents itself, to become aware of the ever-present limitations of capacity, while simultaneously using our awareness in a compassionate manner to nourish and transform others.

Payoff for being helpful can be short- or long-term; it can be quid pro quo or generalized and abstract. Sharing information with other birders on rare bird locations or identification challenges is likely to be reciprocated, and it can become the basis of firm friendships. Larger efforts extend benefits from individuals we know or hope to know to people we will never meet in person and to other creatures as well. By volunteering our time, and perhaps some financial resources as well, we discover ways of contributing to the future.

Compassion

Compassion is needed for other birders, for non-birders, for all beings and for the earth herself.

To expand our compassion in this manner is clearly not a matter of succumbing to diminished capacity. On the contrary, one can become newly energized and empowered. An opportunity emerges to imbue ourselves with a new sense of purpose that transcends the old focus on building a better lifelist.

Compassion comes from an awakening of the mind. Respecting others, observing, and interrelating comprise the basis of that capacity. Compassion for sentient beings carries the wish for them to be free from suffering. How can compassion be attained? We can take some quiet time each morning to set an intention of awareness for the day, to connect to our environment, friends and family (including birds). An evening time of reflection enables us to review the day and examine whether compassion guided our behavior. Moving from self-absorption to connectedness increases awareness and ability to be in the now.

A capacity for compassion brings a connection from the internal to the external world, a sense of life bringing happiness throughout the day. This interconnectedness in turn increases our abilities to observe and understand what we see in the course of a day. Simple times of reflecting can increase compassion for the environment, the totality of species, family and friends.

The American Indian concept of relatedness of all species is a compassionate view of the world. Respect for the bird and environment comprises a sense of family and connectedness with one's surroundings. The actions of one species affect the lives of others. We give and take here in the moment with our "family" of species.

Do you bird to live or live to bird? Birding can enhance our observational abilities and increase the ability to connect with other aspects of life. Or, birding can consume one's attention through obsession.

Chapter 6

ZEN LIVES OF BIRDS

"A bird flies in the sky, and no matter how far it flies there is no end to the air."
—Zen Master Dogen, *Moon in a Teardrop*

Eastern wisdom instructs us to value the journey over the destination, to see the importance of process over result. At every moment, at every place where we find ourselves, we have arrived after a long journey, and yet we are at home. Birds are excellent teachers of this dynamic. They are at home on their breeding territories; they are at home on their wintering grounds; they are at home on every flyway stopover. "Home" denotes a connectedness that goes beyond familiarity. Home embodies a sense of security much deeper than safety. In their every here, and their every now, birds show us they have arrived at home.

Although many of the vignettes that follow show birds being in the moment, the stories are not in support of any single, simple characterization of birds. Instead, they show birds being skillful, being clumsy, using strategy, communicating, engaging in family dynamics, and simply playing—sometimes, even with species other than their own. Additionally, these vignettes are as much about the perceptions and awareness of birders and other people as they are of birds. They are about what we may see when we look beyond species identification and checklist areas.

Western science often warns of the danger of "anthropomorphizing" birds and animals, that is, attempting to understand them in terms of human behavior, motives and emotions. We are more in need of "zoomorphizing" ourselves than of ridding ourselves of anthropomorphizing other creatures. Another way of stating this is to suggest that in place of a narrowly anthropocentric worldview, we need to develop a broadly biocentric worldview, or understanding from species other than our own.

Anthropomorphism at its worst is the tendency to judge birds by our own standards of morality. Jays are often castigated for their loud, aggressive, brash behavior, and other species attract human ire for similar reasons. A woman who referred to Common Grackles as "jackals" added that they are "a bad bird that chases other birds away." When birds kill other birds, people—including some birders—may refer to it as "murder." A problem with this is that it may prevent us from seeking a more complete understanding of interactions between birds and their environments. For example, consider Barn Swallows: a naïve human understanding is likely to focus on the grace and beauty of the bird, whereas from the perspective of mosquitoes swallows are surely among the most horrific of Demons. The ecological role of Barn Swallows is undoubtedly far more complex than the simple conclusions that would be quickly drawn by humans or mosquitoes.

A common human folly is to think that we know what others are thinking, whether or not the others are human. We may be wrong in what we ascribe to bird behavior, yet there is a parallel danger, the danger of dismissing sentient behavior as mere programming and stimulus-response. If we dismiss recognition of their sentient behavior as mere "anthropomorphism," we diminish our own humanity as well as the vitality of birds.

Sentient Beings

The young Ravens are out of the nest. Three are still in the nest tree, but one is in another tree. The parents are perched on tipi poles nearby, and compared to the last few weeks, when they've been very defensive of the nest, they seem quite relaxed.

It is not anthropomorphism to say this. To deny their earlier defensiveness or their present relief would be to intentionally overlook the nearly universal concern that parents show for their offspring. Not fully universal, to be sure—certain species are inattentive to their young, as are certain human beings. Common Ravens, though, rank among the best of us in the care they lavish on their children.

(June 17, 2005, Santa Fe NM)

Another danger in anthropomorphism is the rush to judgment—characterizing a species based on limited information. If jays seem insensitive, it may be because we have paid insufficient attention to a full gamut of their behavior.

Hawk, Finch, & Jay

A Sharp-shinned Hawk had captured and devoured a House Finch, and now a Western Scrub-Jay was giving loud alarm calls near the pile of feathers. Three Cañon Towhees were cowering along the sidelines. The jay began calling loudly and repeatedly, and dancing a full circle around the feather midden, looking directly at it from one angle and then another. Surely it would be anthropomorphizing to describe this as a jay's reaction to a murder scene, and probably it is anthropomorphizing to have said the towhees were cowering. But few people would hesitate to refer to birds' "alarm" calls, and is it other than factual to talk of a bird being excited? The most elegant explanation of this scene is that the jay recognized what had occurred and found the finch's fate disturbing.

(April 13, 1997, Santa Fe NM)

We need not be interested in birds because they remind us of people. We could just as well be interested in people because they remind us of birds.

The following are candid moments in the Zen lives of birds, most of them taken more-or-less verbatim from field notebooks over the past thirty years, and a few from other sources.

Fortune 500 Owls

In November or December of 1989, employees of a Fortune 500 company in Southern California discovered a female Great Horned Owl sitting on a nest in a pine tree on the east side of the four-story administrative office building. The nest was roughly at the third floor ceiling level, and at the time, fourth-floor cubicles had been removed for reconstruction associated with a departmental reorganization. This provided a large open space where Company employees were able to gather and observe the owls, without disturbing working employees. During high points of interest there were often more than twenty people crowded into the room watching the owls. At least several hundred employees visited on occasion. The nest had been built and used by American Crows early in 1989.

Just when the owls took over the nest was a matter of dispute. Some company porters claimed to have seen the owl on the nest before Thanksgiving, but a financial analyst insisted she had discovered the owl in December and showed it to the porters.

At least one chick seems to have hatched on January 25th or 26th. Corporate Communications began taking photographs for the company newspaper. There were two chicks by February 1st, and three chicks were seen on the ninth. As the young owls grew rapidly, the nest began getting visibly crowded and crows began harassing the owls. Employee attentions began shifting from more-or-less objective observations and comments to expressions of anxiety about the owls' well-being. Key concerns were that the nest was too small, that the mother owl was being inattentive to the babies' safety, and that the father owl was providing insufficient food.

One young owl fell from the nest on February 26. It was rescued by a company biologist and taken to a wildlife rehabilitation facility recommended by one of the porters. Corporate Communications issued a mild rebuke; they would've preferred bringing in a cherry picker and filming the return of the owl to the nest. A second young owl fell on March 5, and it too was taken to the rehab center despite pleas from Corporate Communications to restage the capture.

Some were relatively straight-forward observations of behaviors that people had never had opportunity to observe, such as young owls swallowing small rodents.

▸ Woman: "Oh, look, she's feeding it something. Ooh, it's all hairy. What do you suppose it is? Oh, my god, look, he swallowed it whole!"

Man: "Reminds me of some people I know."

▸ Woman: "Owls steal crow's nests. They don't build their own. That's why the crows keep hanging around. They just want their nest back."

▸ Second woman: "Well, of course. Can you blame them?"

Others were clearly anthropomorphic renderings of challenges faced by the owls, challenges that echoed concerns in the lives of the employees themselves. Several categories of concern, with sample comments, were as follows:

Corporate productivity and "credit"

Relatively little attention was given to this topic. When it was, it was initiated by older men, and often with sarcasm. Company supervisors and managers were notably absent from the crowd of owl observers.

▸ Man: "Somebody's missing an opportunity. They should be charging admission."

▸ Woman: "I guess I'd better get back to work. But you've gotta admit, this is more interesting than the merger."

(Elevator conversation):

▸ Woman: "Oh, I'm bright-eyed and bushy-tailed this morning. Just glad to be here."
Man, clapping another man on the shoulder: "That's like this guy. He's got a good job, watching those owls out the fourth floor window."

▸ A man asked the porter who took the young owl to rehab, "Are they giving the company credit?" The porter was a bit confused by this, and said well, they would probably mention the company, and the man said, "The company should get some benefit from this—publicity, or something. I mean, with all the attention being given to these owls, and the amount of time people are spending watching them and fooling around with them..."

‣ A group of us went into the observation room. "Come to check on the owls, eh?" asked one man. "Well, we want to hear the clink of cash when you go in there." Everyone laughed, and a man in our group said, "I thought you wanted folding money!"

Cuteness

‣ Woman: "I was over a little before seven this morning, and the Daddy was here, too. They were both there at the edge of the nest with the babies all gathered around, everybody snuggling. It was so sweet!"

‣ One young woman had color prints of the owls that she'd taken with a 200 mm lens. She showed them around just like, on other occasions, she's shown pictures of her stepchildren.

‣ Woman: "Oh, look, he's looking right at us. Oh, isn't he cute? Look what beautiful eyelashes he has."

‣ Woman: "Oh, isn't he adorable! I'd just love to hug and squeeze him."

‣ Late in the afternoon, Ed and Steve came into the office, laughing. Steve said they were looking at the owl, "…and he saw us, and started bobbing his head from side to side—and we're both a couple of big kids! Ed started moving his head side to side, and I moved mine up and down, and the owl kept going side to side so I changed and went side to side too!" Steve could hardly tell the story for laughing, and both he and Ed illustrated their movements. Ed also put on a funny facial expression of bug-eyed curiosity which made the birder think this was no mere response to the owl, but a deep imitation – to some extent, a magical moment of trans-species identification.

Adequacy of nest/housing

‣ Bob: "I don't see how they're going to make it, as big as

they're getting, and as small as that nest is."

▶ Ed and Bob began discussing the size of the nest as we went over to check on the owls. To Bob's comment, Ed responded, "I'll bet your son thinks his room is too small." Bob "His room? He fills the whole house!" Ed: "You know, my parents are still in the same house where I grew up. It's only a thousand square feet, and there were five of us. What's the square footage of your house?" Bob: "Twenty-four hundred. Yeah, I suppose it's all relative."

▶ Man: "Have you seen the owls today? That nest is really getting too small for them."

▶ Man (after the second owlet fell from the nest): "That's what I expected, all along. That nest was just too small. I think this one will make it, now."
▶ Man: "There were just too many people in that nest."

Parental care/skills/devotion/indulgence of and sentimentality about children

▶ Woman: "They're so cute! But they're so big! What do they eat? She can't leave them there. Don't they eat anything?"
  Man: "Daddy does the hunting. He brings them mice and gophers." The man pointed out the adult male in the nearby tree. It took the woman a while to see him; then she said, "Huh! He's not hunting. He's asleep, and she's doing all the work!"

▶ "Marilyn" came over to report that a young Great Horned Owl was perched out on a limb while the mother was in the nest. "I can't believe it!" she fumed, "What kind of mother is she? No wonder the other two fell out of the nest!"
  The biologist, Ed, explained that the nest is too small and

that he knew "from the beginning" that they wouldn't all "make it." Marilyn listened but stuck by her indignation. "I don't think she knows what she's doing." Marilyn pressed on with her character flaw theory. "I was over there last week, before the second one fell out of the nest, and she had planted herself right in the middle of the nest while the babies were teetering on the edge. What a bitch!"

▸ Man: "Mama owl looks almost relieved now, with only two little guys to take care of."
▸ Man: "The mama owl is gone. The kid is in the nest, but she's nowhere in sight. Do you think she'll come back? Or did she just decide, 'Okay, kid, you're on your own, now?'"

▸ Woman: "If I'd had three babies, I'd probably fly away too."

▸ Man: "I wonder where Mama was yesterday? I guess it's like with all parents. Sometimes you've just got to get away."

▸ Man: "We're in training now. She's learning to fly and her parents are keeping an eye on her." (Many, though not all, women have been calling the owlets "she." Lately, I've noticed several men, including the biologist, saying "she." Does it possibly have to do with this owlet's perceived vulnerability, being out of the nest but still unable to fly?)

▸ Steve: "It's like I told the birder, eh? It's gonna be fly or die!" "No," Ed said, "it's going to be alright."

▸ Man: "I guess he was kind of awkward and sort of crash-landed into the branches, but he is flying."

▸ Bob was very pleased to hear that the young owl is flying (he was out of the office Monday and Tuesday so had just learned about it). His pride was palpable, reminiscent of when his son began walking a few years earlier.

▸ A woman announced that she's planning to visit the owls at the Tujunga Wildlife Station. She talked to someone there who said one of the youngsters had made his first kill, a mouse that made the mistake of wandering into the cage.

Gender issues
▸ Woman: "I wonder where the father is?"
▸ Woman: "So where is the Daddy all this time? Probably off sleeping or beating up on crows. I hope he's hunting and bringing them food once in a while."

General safety/well-being issues (weather, predators)
▸ Man: "That weekend rainstorm was something! I was afraid the nest would get waterlogged and fall apart, or bring the branch down."

▸ Woman: "I was so worried about them before. Especially when we had that storm. But they're big enough now, I think they'll make it."

▸ Second woman: "Yeah, unless the crows get them. Or a cat. I've worried about a cat climbing up there and getting them."

▸ Third woman: "No, I think that's too high. A cat wouldn't be able to get back down."

▸ Marilyn was expressing specific fears that if the remaining owlet fell to the ground, cats would get it. Ed and the birder tended to think the owlet would be capable of defending itself from a cat.

Environmental arguments

▸ With two owlets having fallen from the nest and the third awkwardly climbing around outside the nest, Marilyn was urging the biologist to capture the remaining bird. Ed declined and began talking about natural selection. This provoked an argument. "It's nature's way," he said. Another woman in the room took Marilyn's side and said, "It isn't nature, if we're watching. We're involved now, and we can't just pretend we aren't."

▸ Marilyn came back to our office a few minutes later and began fussing at Ed. Bob, hearing her, was annoyed. "Don't you just love it? Here she's all worried about this one little owl, but every weekend she and her husband are out there raping the desert with their off-road vehicles!"

Marilyn and Ed have argued about the desert before, and she tried to use this in her argument. "I don't understand you," she said. "You get so upset about the turtles out there in the desert, and there are fifty million of them. But here you've got one little baby owl you could do something about, and you just sit there!"

▸ Ed kept trying to argue natural selection. Steve chimed in on Ed's side, saying, "We don't want to end up with owls that let their babies fall out of nests." Ed attempted to turn Marilyn's own argument against her: "See, you're the one that keeps saying she's an unfit mother. If I believed that, I wouldn't want to rescue any of them—keep them out of the gene pool! But I don't think that's it. I just think they're inexperienced, and they'll probably do better next time."

Marilyn remained unswayed. Ed told her, "Try to be objective about this," but she retorted, "You're mean!"

▸ Marilyn: "I just hate to see little things die."

Ed: "I know, I used to feel like that, too, but I came around. If they can't make it without human help, it's better not to have them out there."

Marilyn: "I won't come around. I'm afraid. I want my grandchildren to be able to see these things, and not just in a zoo."

Were company employees merely goofing off, "fooling around" with the owls? In reflecting on the situation, the birder was struck by the widespread employee enthusiasm for these owls, compared to pervasive low morale and gloom about the company. The owls provided a few weeks of respite during a time of high corporate stress (an attempted merger, ultimately unsuccessful, was being pursued).

It was striking that people in the company's administrative rank and file seemed able to more closely identify with the life struggles of a family of owls than they could with motivations of the men who controlled the company.

SYMBIOSIS

Zen birding focuses attention on the relationships in an ecosystem, shifting the center from our own. Gardening is a nature-connecting activity. Every yard requires some of this planning and planting. There is a choice. Will the yard be a food resource and a haven for birds, and some nutritious plants for you as well? Imagine landscaping as habitat, those small patches for food and perch in human populated environments. This habitat can meet your needs and bring daily joy as well. Tending plants connects us to the seasons.

Learning the favored berries and food sources of bird species in your area from other birders or from nurseries can foster the path to conscious planting. Instead of pesticiding away insects in your yard, think of them as a scrumptious treat for certain species of birds. Your visitors will be grateful.

Planting trees provides perches and nesting habitat. Our yard in Santa Fe had a small organic garden on one end and birdbaths on the other. Even trimmed branches were not discarded. We piled them high for quail habitat. A little thought in daily living can provide abundance to our feathered relations.

The Story Of Binky

In mid-December of 2001, a Greater Roadrunner began stalking our Santa Fe bird feeders. Despite his best efforts, though, the Roadrunner was luckless. The little birds were too cautious and always flew off before he got close. Over the next few weeks, the Roadrunner became a regular resident in the yard, sometimes stalking birds, but most often seen huddled down in our compost bin as if enjoying the scant warmth from decomposing food scraps and yard waste. We began calling him "Binky."

One day in January, I disturbed Binky as he sat in the compost bin, and then I disturbed a mouse. When the mouse made a run for it, Binky set off in quick pursuit. He grabbed the mouse by the tail, beat it against the ground a few times, and then swallowed it whole. The Roadrunner learned quickly to associate me with mouse treats.

Once in early February, I found Binky on the patio, and called to him, "Binky, you want a mouse?" Binky cocked his head as if listening, and I repeated: "Come on, Binky, let's go find a mouse!" Binky won the race to the compost bin, waiting on the nearby rock wall. I began probing the pile with a stick. Binky trembled with anticipation and made a couple of false starts toward the bin. Either he has an active imagination or he saw something I didn't. A mouse finally appeared, and Binky nabbed it. It was a big one, and Binky had to work at subduing it. He took it over under the juniper tree to finish it off.

In March of 2002, Binky began cooing from the rooftop of the house, calling for a girlfriend, and not long afterwards one appeared. She followed him around the yard for a while, and then they both disappeared. I wondered if she decided his taste in snacks was a bit too gross, but mostly I was just grateful for his past assistance in mouse population control.

Late in the year, Binky returned. At the time, there were no mice in the compost bin, but every time I went out, Binky watched and waited. Roadrunners are not known for their patience, and there certainly was no personal loyalty. Finding no mice in the compost bin, Binky soon left for parts unknown. It had been an ideal symbiosis, while it lasted. We were happy to get rid of the mice, and Binky benefited from undertaking the task for us.

(December 21, 2002, Santa Fe NM)

The Fugitives: Great Horned Owls

For the past four days I had not seen the owls. For two days before that, and on and off in the weeks prior, they had perched in the big willow, first here, then there, enduring an irregular barrage of harassment by birds large and small —ravens, crows, a magpie, jays, robins and even chickadees and titmice.

But this morning, when I walked into the studio office, I looked out the window and my eyes met those of a Great Horned Owl perched on the rim of the birdbath.

As I watched, the owl waded into the birdbath, then dipped its head furtively into the water and drank. After several quick drinks, the owl hunkered down, briefly immersed its face and breast in the water and, shaking itself vigorously, took a quick bath. Then, the second owl joined the first. Both perched on the birdbath, and both looked nervously one way and then the other. The second owl drank a few times, and then hopped down to the ground. After about fifteen minutes, during which I took a few photos of the lingering owl, both had departed.

It is clear to me that the owls are continually persecuted by other birds. As a matter of adaptation, they stay in any given roost spot only a few days until too many of their foes have discovered them; then, they become fugitives, and move on to the next brief haven.

(November 18, 2000, Santa Fe NM)

Choosing To Trust: Great Horned Owl

First thing this morning, I turned on the garden hose to refill the birdbaths. One Great Horned Owl was in a piñon fairly close to the house. It took flight, but joined its mate in a cluster of piñons and junipers down slope, below the rock terraces. Both watched as I refilled the birdbath where they bathed yesterday. I turned off the water and went into the studio, and at 7:25 a.m., one of the owls came to the birdbath. It stayed for nearly fifteen minutes, occasionally drinking, keeping a wary eye out for jays and robins and looking occasionally at me,. The second owl did not come to the birdbath but went directly to the big willow.

(November 19, 2000, Santa Fe NM)

DANCING

Being with birds can bring a new sense of freedom. A friend once remarked, "I feel such freedom with birds, as though I could fly, even soar in life."

Eastern Kingbird

An Eastern Kingbird, doing a dance in apparent celebration of the twilight. The lake as his stage, beginning high above and moving higher, hovering, twittering, stalling and falling, dipping and rising, taking an impromptu break to grab a bite to eat—a twirling dashing plunge at a convenient hapless insect—and then back to the dance. Alone tonight. On previous nights I've seen two birds dancing together.

The Eastern Kingbirds' dusk dance comes a bit later every night — tonight, shortly after 8:50 p.m.

(June 9 and 11, 1976, Round Lake, Savona NY)

Common Raven

While walking the greenbelt, I came across a Common Raven— probably a juvenile—'dancing' on a housetop television antenna, apparently fascinated by the noise it made, squeaking and clanging against a chimney spark guard.

(July 6, 2001, Santa Fe NM)

INDEPENDENCE FROM HUMAN MISFORTUNE

Obsession leads to distractive brain chatter, in turn leading to suffering. Breathe in, breathe out. Expand awareness of the beauty around you. Zen birding releases the mind, relieves the suffering of life.

House Sparrow

Avian life goes on as usual amidst human woes. Several pairs of House Sparrows are exploring for nesting sites under the tiles on the roof of a house half smashed by a mudslide, and also in the ruined debris which was once the rear portion of the house. Up the slope, a Northern Mockingbird is singing deliriously and doing an aerial dance from a television antenna atop a house which mudslides

had broken away last week.
(February 24, 1980, Monterey Park CA)

Rock Wren

At Fort Union National Monument, on the Santa Fe Trail, I was astonished to find historical exhibits praising the bravery of nineteenth century American soldiers and the fortitude of their wives, yet dismissing Indians as people who fought simply "to prove their manhood." The exhibits said nothing about the Apache homeland having been invaded by hordes of American merchants and settlers who discarded trash along the trail and killed the game animals upon which Apache people depended for their subsistence.

I walked outside and heard a melancholy yet reassuring song—a Rock Wren, singing from the top of a crumbling adobe wall, the remnant of a fireplace in a military officer's former home. It seemed fitting that this Rock Wren was here, singing on behalf of dozens of generations of his own ancestors, and to my ears, at least, also singing on behalf of the Jicarillas with whom Rock Wrens gracefully shared this landscape—this landscape that the Americans considered so desolate, yet fought so desperately to control.
(June 20, 2005, Fort Union National Monument NM)

Carolina Wren

In the aftermath of hurricanes Ivan (September 2004, which scored a direct hit on Pensacola) and Katrina (August 2005, striking only a glancing blow on Pensacola), effects on avian activity were difficult to assess. A month after Ivan's 135-mph winds swept across Pensacola, human inhabitants were still reeling from the damage. But Carolina Wrens started the morning in song and continued singing all day. A wren ducked into a tangle of broken branches full of dead leaves, up in a big live oak tree. A pair of wrens chased each other up and over and around an enormous broken stump, singing bubbly songs all the while. A wren explored an open trash bag filled with branches; and a wren dashed through a ruined greenhouse. In the reckonings of wrens, human losses become exciting new places ripe for investigation.

(October 14, 2004, Pensacola FL)

SKILL

Our practice can transform us; things are not fixed in this life. When in touch with one's body, not just the mind, all senses are enhanced. Zen birding does not set us apart, species from species.

Red-tailed Hawk

...soaring low over the woods, facing into the snow and the westerly wind, stalling against it, motionless, for ten to fifteen seconds, turning and riding with it for more than fifty yards, and then once again wheeling around to face into it.

(January 14, 1976, Ontario, New York)

Black-throated Green Warbler

A female, in the ailanthus tree, flitted from branch to branch or, more accurately, from branch to midair and back to branch. In midair the bird hovered, twisted and turned, snapping up flying insects that, despite the still brisk and gusty breezes, are abundant in small swarms around the tree.

(Oct 2, 1975, Rochester, NY)

DEFENDING THE NEST

Life is not about stability or the constant. Changes, moment to moment, teach us the lessons of impermanence.

Song Sparrow

Perched on a post in the old grape arbor, softly but persistently giving an alarm chip in protest of my nearby presence; with a mouthful of food, waiting, hopping about, flying to nearby bushes in an effort to divert or discourage me. Finally, after 10 minutes of being literally devoured by mosquitoes, I am indeed discouraged.

...A pair of Song Sparrows, angry and indignant because, apparently, I'm near their nest. It seems, so I think now, having walked about 15' into the margin of the woods with only one bird still following me and fussing persistently from a series of perches within five to eight feet of me, that their tactic is to distract by going the other direction from the nest itself. Yes! Going back, I find the second bird perched in a sumac rising above the red-osiers with a mouthful of caterpillars. I must have been with arm's length of the nest. The pair distracted me in every possible direction for 20 minutes, but I couldn't find the nest. Eventually, admiration and pity triumphed over curiosity and I gave up my search.

(May 31, 1976, Ontario NY)

Blue Jay

A nest about 5.5' above the ground in a small pine tree; roughly constructed with coarse twigs; four blue eggs with purplish speckling most pronounced at the ends. The jay is not by any means an ardent defender of the nest—a surprising thing, given the brash and vocal nature of jays. The bird sitting on the nest fled when I was about fifteen feet away and watched, relatively quietly, from a distant tree until I went on. (2001, Santa Fe. NM)

INEPTITUDE

Letting go of obsession is the path to perception. Only then, can we let go of perfection.

Cedar Waxwing

When I was a child, there were several tall American holly trees in our yard, and when the trees were young they had abundant berry crops. In late winter and early spring, flocks of waxwings would gorge themselves on the fermenting berries until some of the birds were so inebriated that they would fall to the ground.

(1950s, Pensacola FL)

Evening Grosbeak

This morning I watched as a male grosbeak played "King of the Mountain" with two cowbirds at the feeder. He consistently won out, but twice he took sudden flight for no obvious reason, and each time flew straightaway into the windowpane. It didn't seem to phase him, though. Each time he bounced off the window like a tennis ball and without missing a wingbeat continued flying in the opposite direction.

(April 1, 1976, Round Lake, Savona NY)

Red-tailed Hawk

Watched the kill of a Beechy ground squirrel (Citellus beecheyi) and was surprised at the hawk's fumbling. Working close to the ground,

the hawk made several passes at the squirrel before the catch was made, and the squirrel was briefly outrunning the hawk.
   (February 26, 1980, Chino CA)

Steller's Jay

Watched a Steller's Jay dive out of a big yellow pine and attempt to capture a moth fluttering along about two feet above the ground. The jay missed the moth, jumped back up from the ground and snapped at the moth, missing again. The moth fled, flying low (a few inches off the ground), but the jay cornered it again about ten feet away—tried again to catch it, but missed. Then another jay interceded. This jay also missed, and during a brief altercation between the two jays, the moth made a successful escape.
   (August 8, 1983, Chula Vista Campground, Mt. Pinos CA)

Great Horned Owl

Teenagers can be clumsy—no matter what their species. One of the juvenile owls was in the middle of the road when I drove up at 9:30pm. It fled to a roadside juniper and perched there, screeching; another was screeching farther down toward the greenbelt. I had been in the house only a short time when there was a horrendous noise on the roof. One of the owls either attempted a capture or simply tried to land on the roof. There was a sudden squealing of talons on metal, along with shrieks of surprise and flapping of wings against the roof. Then, as suddenly as it started, there was silence.
   (August 2, 2001, Santa Fe NM)

INNOVATION
Letting go can lead to innovation.

Herring Gull

Taking a mussel shell in its beak, a gull will slowly climb up, hover for a single wingbeat, tilt forward and drop the shell. The gull then stalls, turning head down to follow the shell as it plummets groundward, and then dives in pursuit. The height from which the shell is dropped varies—sometimes only ten or fifteen feet, but if the shell doesn't break on the first try the gull will take it higher for the next drop. I didn't observe any gulls dropping shells from more than about thirty feet.

(November 7, 1976, Revere/Winthrop, north of Boston MA)

Horned Lark

I spotted a small bird at the upper edge of the snow bank alongside the road, stopped, recognized it as a Horned Lark, rolled down the window for a better look, and began seeing more of them. What had appeared at first to be lumps of dirt in the snow were, in fact, more Horned Larks. Each bird—there were 12 in all—had hollowed out a cavity in the snow, a small windbreak or snow cave. One took added advantage of a large lump of snow, fashioning its shelter in a natural depression behind it. The cavities were no deeper than the height of the hunched-down birds, yet I imagine even this minimal shelter gives a good amount of protection from the wind—a particularly important consideration in weather this wet and cold (temperatures ranged from 18 to 27 degrees F. today). Cavities were more or less randomly placed along the sloped edge of the snow bank, which is 1.5 to 2' high. Some were near the top and others only inches from the road surface. None was closer than 6" apart, and most were about 1' apart. My presence had an effect on the birds. They began stirring around when I stopped the car, and several hopped out of their snow shelters and stood nearby regarding me with caution or curiosity. A twittered murmuring was briefly heard, and then the birds began settling back into their windbreaks. A couple of them never moved except to turn their heads around to look.

(January 10, 1977, near U. Mass. campus, Amherst MA)

DISTRACTION
There is silence when struggle ceases.

Red-winged Blackbirds
Two males were engaged in aerial combat over the lake, their acrobatics ending with one chasing the other toward the house. But then both of them suddenly stopped at the feeding area on the sidewalk and ate together peaceably for several minutes.

(May 18, 1976, Round Lake, Savona NY)

Western Scrub-jay
Two Western Fence Lizards were scurrying up the trunk of a pine tree when suddenly a Western Scrub-jay swooped down and nabbed one of the lizards. The jay went to the ground, pecked the lizard a couple of times, and then flew off carrying its prey.

(April 28, 1991, Rancho Santa Ana Botanic Garden, Claremont CA)

What do we do once we've seen more than half of the birds recorded in our home state? Some birders go into a lethargic state, similar to birds during the midday doldrums. Others begin chasing after every rare bird reported in their state, working to raise their state list to seventy or eighty percent or more. Still others begin working on a list for another state, or they work toward a big national or continental list. Some who can afford to do so begin working on a worldwide life list. But then there are those who begin looking in more depth into the ecosystem they know best—learning the trees, shrubs and flowers; insects, reptiles and amphibians; mammals; and the seasons and interactions of them all. Some get more involved in conservation issues, working toward preservation of habitat for the familiar birds they love.

Chapter 7

CONNECTEDNESS AND NATURE

"We are always in relationship to something. It is in discovering a wise and compassionate relationship to all things that we find a capacity to honor them all."
Jack Kornfield, *A Path With Heart.*

Birders do act, in many ways, just like predators. We stalk birds. We talk among ourselves about wanting, needing, getting or having gotten a bird. We look directly at them (often with enormous shiny eyes), and our body language is not entirely unlike that of a cat about to pounce.

It's no wonder, then, that birds tend to flee from us. True, we birders don't intend to eat them, but this planet's many creatures have some difficulty deciphering one another's intentions. Even among others of our own species, we can judge intentions only by observing behaviors.

There is something to be said for that old and nearly outmoded term, "birdwatchers." A gentler, less aggressive term, it harkens back to a time when those who looked at birds did so in a bit more passive manner. The term suggests some considerations even for those who are, indeed, "birders."

The next time you're looking for birds without much success, try stopping and standing still, like a tree. The birds may come to you—or they may not. Either way, the experience can be instructive. Connectedness is an ever-present awareness of environment.

BEING IN THE MOMENT

One thing we can clearly see, in closely observing birds, is how utterly skillful they are in being in the present moment. A bird's emotions can run a complete gamut, from serenity to panic, and back to sedate calm, in a matter of seconds. A bird can be precisely where she is, not where she remembers herself having been or where she imagines herself to be in the future. Before any appreciable awareness of Zen consciousness reached American shores, Charlton Ogburn (*The Adventure of Birds*) wrote, "Probably nothing makes it more difficult to put ourselves in a wild animal's place than the narrowness of its awareness span. ...for our fellow beings the light is a beam of a width measurable in seconds. They live in the present to a degree probably unimaginable to us." Avian awareness is indeed narrowly focused in space-time, yet it has depth in other dimensions. Caring, connectedness, and release from obsession are part of the practice.

Awareness

Shortly before dawn, I walk toward the "rising" sun at a moderate clip—roughly half a mile per hour. But in truth, the sun is not rising. Instead, this part of the earth's surface is rolling out of darkness and into a view of the sun at the rather amazing speed (here in northern New Mexico) of more than six hundred miles an hour. Without effort, I cling to the earth's surface; with concentration, I can perceive her movement. If I sit still and meditate on the rotation, I get a just-barely-perceptible sense of falling forward toward the sun.

But meanwhile, the sun hurtles around the outer edge of the Milky Way Galaxy at the dizzying rate of nearly ten thousand miles per minute, and the entire galaxy is moving at nearly twelve thousand miles per minute relative to other galaxies in the local group. These movements I cannot perceive, no matter how I might try.

I turn my attention back, now, to the birds, singing their morning greetings to the sun. They sing without calculation or concern for what is moving in which direction, or how fast—and yet they are vastly more aware than I am, of the moment-to-moment consequences of earth's movements.

(June 9, 2005, Santa Fe NM)

Mallard

In shallow water just above the falls: a pair, mating. This seemed a most inopportune choice of locations. The current threatened to sweep them off into the main stream. Disengaging by necessity as they floated toward the edge, they showed complete disregard of the abyss, preening themselves, dunking and flapping, preening some more, and then climbing onto a rock to dry off.

(June 17, 1975; Dufferin Island Nature Trail, Niagara Falls, Ontario, Canada)

White-throated Swift

Observed a pair mating. High in the air, they locked each other in an embrace that sent them both plummeting groundward, spinning like a maple seed. They either misjudged their position vis-à-vis the canyon rim, or in the heat of passion simply took no notice, and they landed with a slight thud on the rock overhang at the canyon's edge. The spinning movement sent one of the swifts skidding under a ledge. The bird emerged seconds later looking a bit shaken, only to launch itself promptly over the edge back into the canyon. The second bird spun off in the other direction, but took wing directly. Both back in the air, the pair began mating once again.

(June 28, 1981; Chapin Mesa, Mesa Verde National Park CO)

INTERSPECIES COOPERATION

Recognizing our place in the environmental chain of beings inspires us. Conscious birding becomes a practice. An everyday way of being and acting in the universe emerges.

Cooper's Hawk

A Cooper's Hawk was in a bare-branched tree along with a mixed-species mob-in-waiting—including Western Kingbird, Phainopepla, Bullock's Oriole, and House Finches. The birds in the mob seemed generally unexcited, but from time to time one would venture out to peck or make a close pass at the hawk—almost as if "counting coup".

(May 27, 2002, Percha Dam State Park, NM)

Chestnut-sided Warbler

A male Chestnut-sided Warbler, resplendent in his bright plumage—white breast and belly, rusty red flanks, chartreuse cap and black eye stripe—darted out of the underbrush in the north woods of Maine and followed a large mammal. The warbler began "fly-catching", taking mosquitoes on the wing, from the cloud of insects attending the mammal's passage.

The big mammal stopped, looked at the little warbler, and egocentrically assumed the bird was curious about him—but then, noticed what was actually happening. This mammal was no moose, rather, a human birder suddenly realizing how similar his presence in the woods was to that of a moose or deer from the perspective of an insectivorous little bird.

(July 10, 2004, Caribou ME)

STRATEGY

Strategy without effort comes from peaceful mind and spontaneity, from knowing. The rewarding strategy comes from discovery, rather than from a place of struggling.

Red-tailed Hawk

About 3:00 p.m., three White-tailed Deer were browsing near the edge of the woods at the west side of the fields when a Red-tailed Hawk perched in the top of a tall sapling about a hundred feet from them. The hawk watched intently, looking primarily in the direction of the deer, which continued to move about as before. After perhaps three minutes the hawk swooped down to the ground, landing only about fifteen feet from the deer. All three noticed the movement. Two stepped back rather nervously but the third and closest stepped around a clump of bushes and timidly approached the hawk, craning its neck for a better view. Apparently having decided there was nothing to be alarmed about, the deer nonetheless watched, intently, until the hawk came up out of the deep grass and flew off to the north. Apparently the hawk's strategy was simply to watch closely until the deer startled some unfortunate small rodent out into the open, and then move in and make the kill.

(February 25, 1976, Ontario, NY)

Black-billed Cuckoo

The bird was silent. I was fortunate to have seen it alight in the top of a maple, subsequently dropping from one perch to another (suddenly, without a sound), and from each new perch looking all around (for caterpillars, no doubt). The cuckoo seemed focused on its hunt, and oblivious to me. At the closest, it came within about fifteen feet of me.

(July 31, 1975, 5.55 a.m., Ontario, New York)

TERRITORIALITY
Protect for the moment.

American Crow

It appears that the Holyoke Range—or, more specifically, Mt. Tom—is a boundary between two crow territories. Crows seen north of Mt. Tom are flying south in the morning; those south are flying north. If crows schedule their flights for arrival at the roost around sunset (only an assumption), then the roost area must be some distance on beyond Westfield.

Shortly after 6 a.m., two American Crows are perched in treetops on the southeast slope of Mt. Tom. These two probably spent the night here... do crows have "border guards?"

(February 18 and 21, 1977, Mt. Tom and Interstate 91, between Northampton and Springfield MA)

Gray Catbird

Again, I was confronted by the catbirds. They fussed ever louder. With a bit of imagination on my part, one gave the cry "Quit! Quit!" and the other, "Go 'way!" They alternated: "Quit!" "Go' way!" "Quit!" "Go' way!" becoming more emphatic until in fact I did go away.

(June 25, 1975, along the Genessee River, Rochester, NY)

Communication
A yellow warbler's
Song: Ten thousand times as large
As the bird himself.

Killdeer
A field with a dozen or so pairs of nesting birds. We got out and were given a display of "broken wings," other assorted feigned injuries, and very sad and plaintive wailing.
(June 14, 1975, Montezuma NWR)

TAKING REFUGE
There is refuge in the awakened nature of connectedness. Refuge is not about separation. Being aware of the refuges of other beings connects us.

Common Yellowthroat
A male flitted around the stern of the trawler, rested briefly in the port side net, then flew off to the east, but returned and perched in the outspread wings of the starboard net until 2:25 p.m., when he began hopping around the stern deck. Saw him catch a moth resting in the tangled stern line.

The Yellowthroat has adopted us. He makes brief forays out, circling his new home. He perches for a while on the door chains out on the outrigger, but returns again and again to the area around the stern post, exploring amidst pickstools and baskets and lines, and catching moths. On into Mississippi offshore waters, and he's still with us at 4:30 p.m., and when we stopped at 5 p.m.

Our "mascot," the Yellowthroat, stayed with us as we ran south (after 6:15 p.m.). He abandoned the stern while we set out the rigs. He went and perched on the anchor davit, but afterward, at 7:15 p.m., he perched on a towing cable.

(September 8, 1977, Alabama/Mississippi Gulf of Mexico, shrimp trawler DEBBIE)

REACTION TO STRANGERS AND COMPETITORS

Connection with the environment relieves the mind of suffering. While nature does not judge us, we have the tendency as humans to judge nature. Learning to *be* with nature releases the mind from judgmental patterns.

Northern Mockingbird

For the past two days the mockingbirds have been loudly and persistently fussing, making far more noise than usual, but not singing. The apparent reason is the invasion of migrant sparrows and warblers, which apparently has them feeling threatened. One mocker chased a White-throated Sparrow from a dogwood into a spirea bush, then into the piracantha by the garage, and then into the coral vine thicket by the garden. Another mocker loudly protested the presence of a large flock of warblers, and a few titmice, in the oak tree north of the house. Dogwood berries are a favorite of the mockingbirds. Probably the major focus of their distress is that Northern Cardinals and White-throated Sparrows are also after the berries.

The amount of fussing has decreased in the past few days, as compared to when the White-throated Sparrows and Yellow-rumped warblers first appeared. Apparently the mockers have more or less surrendered to superior numbers, although they have not stopped harassing the warblers and sparrows—it's only a diminishment.

(November 3 and 28, 1977, Pensacola FL)

Caspian Tern, Belted Kingfisher

A Caspian Tern has been flying back and forth along the river all through the afternoon, but a Belted Kingfisher "angrily" chased the big tern away from what is apparently a favorite fishing spot.

(November 21, 1977, Bon Secour AL)

SYMPATHY

Breathe in, breathe out. We are but one in the connectedness of beings. Become one heartbeat with the planet.

Laughing Gull, Herring Gull

About 3 p.m., in the heat of competition for fish scraps being pushed overboard, a 1st year Herring Gull snagged its left wing on our port side towing cable. The bird twisted and turned to no avail, tried to grasp the cable with its beak, but hung there, helpless, for ten minutes or longer. The other gulls—mostly Laughing Gulls—fell silent, lifted up and back from the boat but continued to follow, as if waiting to see the outcome before resuming normal activity. Although we continued pushing scrap fish overboard, only a few immature Laughing Gulls ventured to pick anything up. Finally the Herring Gull managed to twist loose, leaving a few primaries behind. It rested on the water briefly but was flying behind the boat not long afterward, competing for its share of the scraps.

(November 19, 1977, shrimp trawler DON-DAVY, Mobile Bay AL)

THEFT

How to perceive loss, as suffering or acceptance? Loss is loss. Be present to the perception.

Ring-billed Gull, Herring Gull, Red-breasted Merganser, Lesser Scaup

Six immature Ring-billed Gulls and three immature Herring Gulls are gathered around three female Red-Breasted Mergansers, paddling about leisurely and waiting for a merganser to dive and make a catch. Mergansers apparently cannot swallow their prey underwater, and so must bring it to the surface. Yesterday one surfaced six or seven times with the same fish. But there are the gulls, waiting, and unless the merganser dives immediately the gulls will be on top of her trying to wrest the fish away. Given warning—if the gull is several feet away and begins flying toward the merganser—escape is usually effective. But if the merganser makes the mistake of surfacing right alongside a gull or two, its catch is lost.

Mergansers aren't the only victims. Two Ring-billed Gulls and a 1st year Herring Gull teamed up on a Lesser Scaup that had captured a little fish and was trying to swallow it. The scaup held onto his catch through two dives, but when he came up from the third, the Herring Gull deftly snatched the fish out of his bill.

(December 9, 1977, Bon Secour AL)

Northern Goshawk, Common Ravens, a Rabbit and a Coyote

I had just walked under the stone underpass, to the west side of the railroad tracks, when I heard a cry—not a bird, it sounded "like a baby," clearly mammalian. I guessed it to be a rabbit and began quickly walking toward the sound. I looked ahead and saw four Common Ravens converging on a thicket of piñons; then more ravens; and then I spotted a raptor perched in a piñon—a Northern Goshawk, slightly but definitely larger than the ravens that began perching all around the hawk. By the time I saw and identified the hawk, the cries had stopped. Suddenly, a coyote appeared—dashing across the railroad track and into the thicket of piñons beneath the hawk. A couple more cries, then silence, but I could dimly see the coyote taking something in its mouth and then dashing off to the west. It seemed large, possibly a jackrabbit. In all 13 ravens showed up. The raptor flushed and flew, with ravens in half-hearted pursuit.

It was the Goshawk's kill, but the ravens heard the rabbit's cries and hastened to partake of the meal. Then the coyote heard the cries and snatched the rabbit for himself. As soon as the coyote had disappeared with the rabbit, the ravens turned their attention to the hawk. It would be anthropomorphizing to suggest that they were angry about losing the rabbit and hence displaced their emotions against a convenient scapegoat. It is more likely that they would have harassed the hawk regardless, even in the absence of a rabbit or anything else about which to quarrel.

Some may shudder at this tale of what might be called murder, intimidation, and theft. Yet we might instead marvel that the world remains so real, so nearby to the slick pretenses of civilization.

(November 29, 2000, Santa Fe NM)

ADAPTATION

A short attention span might be suspected, or that birds simply are not "greedy." More likely is the search for food as the most important thing for birds.

In other words, survival seems more nearly assured by devotion to the process of seeking food, than by any given actual success in finding food. Of course, birds must actually find and eat food in order to survive. But knowing how to search for food is in the long run more important, as specific food sources eventually run out.

Ladder-backed Woodpecker, Bushtit

Early this afternoon I glimpsed movement deep in the juniper outside the studio window, and with binoculars, I could see that it was a male Ladder-backed Woodpecker, vigorously attacking a mass of mistletoe in the tree. The bird was not merely eating mistletoe berries, or gleaning insects. He was hammering away at the plant, so exuberantly that a small midden of mistletoe branches was piling up beneath the tree.

Despite this resolute attack on the mistletoe, I have no doubt that the woodpecker was indeed taking or seeking nourishment in one way or another. But it set me thinking. Within easy reach there were several feeders with suet, and on other occasions the Ladder-backs— male and female—have availed themselves of the food provided. Yet now, mere inches from a fresh cake of suet, the woodpecker was enthusiastically pursuing an alternative food source.

This is but one example of something noticed of late. Most birds will neither eat until satiated, nor exhaust a given food source. They will, instead, sample it and move on.

Bushtits provide a good example. They appear suddenly, a half dozen or a dozen or two, and they excitedly festoon a suet feeder or a pine cone slathered with peanut butter. Moments later they abandon the first feeder and flock to another. Then they're off again, perhaps to pick through the needles and cones of a piñon somewhere close by. One could follow a flock of Bushtits all day, I'm sure, and although they would never stop eating, they also would never stay more than five minutes or so in any one place.

(November 29, 2000, Santa Fe NM)

FAMILY DYNAMICS

Understanding through connection – by seeing, hearing, and listening – creates relationship. Cyclical time, or life through the seasons, grounds us to family interaction and continuity. We are all relations, connected to each other.

Common Moorhen

A pair, with four fluffy dark gray chicks; the babies already have the black head and red bill. There is no close supervision from the parents. Two chicks were twenty-five feet or more from their mother and even more distant from their father, who was preening and ignoring all the others. One chick began peeping loudly, with no response from its mother. Finally, it joined the second distant chick, and then the two of them went back closer to the mother and the other two chicks.

(July 27, 1975, Montezuma NWR, New York)

Sandhill Crane

One cinnamon-colored immature in a big flock. The flock took flight, including the immature (odd, we thought, only one in such a huge flock; perhaps a late egg!). The youngster promptly fell behind the flock, taking slow laborious wingbeats, much slower and more awkward than the adults. Two adults fell back with him. One led and the other followed. Gradually the immature gained altitude and speed, and the three trailed off after the flock.

(January 16, 1983, Soda Lake, CA)

Scaled Quail

In Santa Fe, the parents would bring their brood to the brick windowsill outside the living room. The babies would line up and peck at their reflections in the window glass, while the parents watched patiently.

(November 5, 2000, Santa Fe, NM)

Red-winged Blackbird

A male Blackbird went down into the hayfield with food in his bill, but came right back out with a youngster in hot pursuit. The two flew over a hundred yards before the male stopped and surrendered the food. A "training flight."

(July 22, 1995, Burns Lake, NM)

Western Scrub-Jay

Two juveniles appeared and were being perfectly competent, taking sunflower seeds from a feeder, and pecking at suet, but when one of the parents showed up, they began begging pitiously, shaking their wings and presenting gawking mouths.

(June 3, 1998, Santa Fe, NM)

Common Raven

As I walked along the railroad tracks shortly before sunset, five Raven youngsters were in one tree, with the parents nearby—one in

169

another tree, and the other perched down on the tracks. The Raven on the tracks flew up and circled around, and moments later I heard the pneumatic horn on a locomotive as it approached the street crossing to the north.

As the train came into sight, the parent in the tree let out a challenging croak and launched directly toward the big engine. Its horn blasted again, drowning out the Raven's vocalizations, but the bird flew straight ahead. The five kids stopped squabbling with each other and craned their necks up, intently watching their parent's attack on the intruder. At the last possible moment, the Raven realized that the locomotive would not be deterred. She wheeled around, and uttered advice to the children while quickly flying back toward them. Three of them heeded her call at once, jumping into the air and flying away from the railroad tracks. One waited for Mom before flying, and one stubbornly stayed in the tree, watching the train with apparent fascination.

(June 18, 2005, Santa Fe, NM)

Raven Parents

Ravens are patient parents. Three are perched atop an ancient Piñon, a parent and two big babies. The youngsters are begging, in high-pitched calls accompanied by much wing-fluttering, "Hraack!' 'Hraack!" ("Feed me! Feed me!")

The parent, facing them, responds to each demand with a low-pitched refusal, "hronk. 'Hronk." ("No. No.")

This interaction is going on as I approach them. It continues as I go on past, and the calls fade into the distance behind me. The demanding cries of the children ascend and descend in little cycles that seem about to degenerate into full-blown tantrums. But the parent's response is steady and unvarying in tone of voice.

(July 1, 2005, Santa Fe, NM)

Today was a day of Raven pedagogy. The nearby family was gathered around our neglected garden today; the kids were mostly being *quiet, apparently listening to the parents.*

But one youngster was distracting his siblings by doing some strange form of Raven yoga—standing atop a spindly fencepost, first on one leg and then the other, all the while stretching one or both wings up, down or out, always in an asymmetric manner, seemingly trying to see how many bizarre poses he could strike without falling over.

Meanwhile, the parents were lecturing. These were not just the usual alarm calls, scolding notes, demands and refusals. There were gurgles and clicks, yawps and yodels, skrecks and sqronks. Can anyone really listen to Ravens and think there is other than language going on?

(July 2, 2005, Santa Fe, NM)

A neighbor recently complained to me about Ravens doing the rumba on her roof.

"Oh," I said, "They're holding classroom sessions. It'll go on all summer, but they'll move from your house before long."

Those of us who like birds often find ourselves defending avian misbehavior, sometimes to no avail. My neighbor was not satisfied and threatened to take a garden hose to them if they kept it up.

I was reminded of this yesterday, seeing one of the Raven families atop yet another house along the greenbelt. We may think our houses belong to us. But in fact (as Raven parents patiently teach), all of these houses are simply part of the Raven-owned landscape: outcroppings of stucco, asphalt and glass, each with its own unique set of resources nearby.

Here there's a birdbath, there an ornamental pool or fountain. Here a compost pile, there a garbage can with a loose lid. Here an old juniper where Great Horned Owls like to roost (and are suscep-tible to harassment), there a cholla cactus patch near a weedy area where House Finches nest and sometimes leave their eggs unguarded. Here a television antenna that bounces and squeaks when perched upon, and over there, a big cottonwood tree with an excellent view of the neighborhood and shade for warm summer afternoons. Ravens can discuss all of this and more, for hours. There are, undoubtedly, many subtleties about resources and diversions that only Ravens understand.

(August 5, 2005, Santa Fe NM)

PLAY

Observing play reminds us of balance, a more natural way of being. Letting go to the pull of playfulness, we are more capable of compassion.

Downy Woodpecker and Dark-eyed (Slate-colored) Junco

A curious "game": a junco and a downy woodpecker repeatedly chasing one another, alternately playing the aggressor. It's hard to see this as other than play. There's no apparent reason for "territorial" considerations at this time of year, and they don't even compete for the same feeder resources. The woodpecker focuses on the suet, the junco on seeds—which are not in the same place.

(February 18, 1976, Ontario, New York)

Barn Swallow

Barn swallows were playing with a white duck feather. One bird had the feather in its mouth and was being chased by two others. The feather was dropped, and the others swooped and chased it down. Then all three chased around. The feather was dropped again. One swallow swooped low and plucked the feather up from the water's surface, fled, and then released the feather again.

(June 11, 1976, Round Lake/Savona, NY)

Red-tailed Hawk and Common Raven

I watched an extended harassment of a Red-tailed Hawk by a Common Raven, beginning at moderate altitude with the Common Raven repeatedly pestering the Red-tailed Hawk. The Red-tailed Hawk climbed higher and higher, but the Common Raven followed every move, generally managing to stay just above the Red-tailed Hawk. The Common Raven was continuously vocalizing, in what seemed to be mocking, taunting tones. Finally, the Red-tailed Hawk lost composure and began screaming with what seemed to be annoyance grading into outrage. Then the Red-tailed Hawk turned on the Common Raven and did a power dive—but this merely seemed to be the whole point of the game for the Common Raven, who managed to stay just out to the Red-tailed Hawk's reach as they both rocketed past me with a loud whoosh of wings, barely thirty feet overhead. Then the Common Raven whirled and turned and was once again above and behind the Red-tailed Hawk, mirroring every move until both were out of sight down Pueblo Canyon.

(March 3, 1999, Santa Fe, NM)

Glaucous-winged Gull

At the airport, a Glaucous-winged Gull repeatedly landing on the cab of a pickup truck only to bounce back into the air, hovering for a few seconds before touching down again—and then settling down on a stainless steel toolbox and prancing back and forth on it.

(April 12, 2005, Seattle-Tacoma International Airport, WA)

DEEP MEMORY

Gary Paul Nabhan, in *Cultures of Habitat: On Nature, Culture, and Story*, described a migrating flock of Great Blue Herons flying parallel to the Lake Michigan shoreline at Gary, Indiana. More precisely, they were following the trace of an interdunal lagoon long buried by blast-iron furnaces, slag heaps and piles of pig iron—"primordial pit stops strung along their ancient migration route" (geological features of the Indiana Dunes, dating back to the last minor glacial advance around ten thousand years ago). Nabhan referred to this as "racial memory."

MYSTERIOUS AND UNEXPECTED BEHAVIORS

The conduct described here undoubtedly has reasonable explanations. What is "mysterious" is when more than one thing is involved, and we are unlikely to ever entirely know what goes on in the minds of creatures so like us and yet so different. For instance, pheasants may be simply warming themselves in the morning sun and nothing akin to appreciation is involved. Yet such things can be difficult or impossible to "test" within a scientific framework, and science can benefit by keeping an open mind in regard to multilevel explanations. In other words, the morning vigil of the pheasants could have functioned to elevate their metabolism, *and* they may have appreciated the role of the sun.

Ring-necked Pheasant

Three pheasants were sitting in small trees watching the dawn with their dark backs and golden bellies glinting in the sun. It seemed as if they were an honor guard paying homage to the dawn. One returned to the cover of the grasses, then another. The third sat still and solitary in the tree for a few moments, but then a second bird returned. Finally, as if on cue, the two came out of the tree and were simultaneously joined by three others, and the five of them flew a swift arc across the field with a whirring of wings.

(March 17, 1975, Ontario, New York)

Northern Cardinal

With the morning light, the cardinals stopped singing. There had been two of them, one in a maple tree here in this yard and one back in the woods or down the street. They had been answering each other phrase by phrase. One wonders: duet, duel, or both?

(August 3, 1975, Ontario, New York)

Pied-billed Grebe

The grebe dunks its breast under first, when beginning to dive; then the tail goes under, leaving only the small head with its rounded beak. A quick glance around: "should I?" and "yes" — under goes the head.

(April 9, 1976, Savona / Round Lake, New York)

Common Raven

Doing a "pajaro loco" routine — tumbling and spinning while falling from high altitude, and making odd croaking noises all the while. I looked in vain for another raven that might've been the object of this display, but no one was in sight.

(May 10, 1996, Santa Fe NM)

Common Raven

A Common Raven flew past, croaking, and then perched on a rock ledge two-thirds of the way up the cliff. There, he acted as if choking, making odd glottalized sounds that were nearly silent — voiceless, it was only the snapping of his throat that I could hear. After a few minutes, he swooped off the ledge, flew toward me, did a sudden full roll to the left so that he was momentarily flying upside down, and then just as quickly rolled back to the right and kept going.

(January 22, 2002, El Morro National Monument NM)

Black-faced Grassquit

The grassquit was perched on the windowsill of a pickup truck, attacking his own image in the rearview mirror. Persistent, he was still at it when I came back around 10 or 15 minutes later. I'm uncertain about the word "attack." The little bird was indeed throwing himself against the mirror, but so gently that it seemed almost as if he wanted contact or communication with the "other bird" rather than wanting him to leave. In fact, he was perched on the rearview mirror itself, occasionally leaning down and softly pecking at the mirror, as if tenderly imploring his reflection to reciprocate.

(July 18, 1993, St. Martin, Leeward Islands)

Black-chinned Hummingbird

Birds sometimes disappoint our stereotypes of them, but if we watch closely, we may discover that they are doing something entirely wonderful.

Today at the Rio Grande Nature Center, Black-chinned Hummingbirds were all but ignoring the sugar-water feeder. Instead, a couple of dozen hummers were darting back and forth over the pond, and hovering alongside the concrete walls of the Visitor Center. People were puzzled. What were the hummingbirds doing?

We may think of Trochilids as strict vegetarians, but they aren't. They need protein in their diets, and the hummers over the water were out catching insects. The ones along the walls of the Visitor Center may have been doing the same thing, or they may have been gathering spider webs to use in nest construction.

People are often astonished that hummingbirds are so aggressive — behavior unbecoming of tiny nectar-eaters, as it were. But if we recognize them for the omnivores that they are, their assertiveness becomes a bit more understandable.

(May 31, 2005, Albuquerque NM)

Shape Shifters

Certain birds are adept at making us a beginner, over and over again. Ravens are particularly good at this. We may encounter a raven and perceive a transitory, shape-shifting personality that lures one into seeing him as other than who he is. Or perhaps, are we correctly seeing an alter-ego she momentarily assumed?

Raven was cruising,
Looked like a black buteo
Primaries spread wide

Raven came flapping
Distant and so determined,
Looking like a crow

Raven went gliding,
Wings tucked back, primaries pinched
—A big black falcon?

Raven in my yard,
Rummaging through the bushes
—A small black dog?

Masters of disguise—
Ravens, revealed by whooshing
wings and croaking calls.

CONCLUSION

LIFE ON EARTH

"Because we all share this small planet earth, we have to learn to live in harmony and peace with each other and with nature. That is not just a dream, but a necessity."
—His Holiness, the IVth Dalai Lama, in his Nobel Peace Prize Lecture

Participating in a community of people who care about life on earth breathes meaning into our existence. *Ahimsa* is the central principle of Buddhist ethics, which calls for doing no harm either to oneself or to others.

Some interpret this narrowly, taking "others" to mean only other humans. Some endeavor to avoid doing active harm, yet they look the other way when it comes to indirect effects of their actions. They also avoid taking responsibility for the actions of others in their community or nation.

Some birders do not want to get involved in conservation efforts, or in "politics." To not get stuck in anger, or depression, over the state of the world and what is happening to nature is important. We can sometimes hold back from action due to fear. Keep in mind the opportunity to learn from birds, in this regard.

The concept of Gaia as Mother Earth, the living breathing organism supporting all life, is important to remember. To worship the earth is not a bad idea, but we need to be clear about what this means. According to the Buddha, worship is really quite simple, but much misunderstood. To worship something is to fulfill our duty to it. Thus, we need to define our duty to the earth and fulfill that duty. As Alan Tennant points out in *On the Wing*, awareness of ecosystems is essential for our contribution to the survival of species.

Once again, we need to come back to awakening and being aware of reality. Birders are good at apprehending the reality of birds that we see in the moment, but there are two crucial ways in which we imagine things to be unlike the way they actually are. One is that we imagine things to be better than they are; the other is when we imagine things to be irredeemably worse than they really are.

The "optimists" think our North American wood warblers are always going to come back every spring in the same sorts of numbers that they've always come back in the past. These people are not looking at the realities of population growth in the tropics, deforestation, the loss of winter habitat, and the fact that those beautiful little birds, when they go south for the winter, must have food and shelter so they can come back in the spring. These often are the people who get upset and angry when environmental organizations want them to contribute to habitat preservation or to lobby for additional protection of birds. On the contemporary scene, protecting birds is a lot more than just keeping people from shooting them. It's also making sure that they have places to live.

On the other side of the coin, there are "pessimists", birders who are not facing reality when they simply give up on the situation. They "awfulize" it. They say deforestation is happening at this rate and population growth is happening at that rate. Then there's global warming, and there's nothing we can do about it. All is lost, and I'm certainly glad that I'm living in the late twentieth century, early twenty-first century, when I still have the opportunity to see all of these hundreds and thousands of species of birds. It's too bad that my grandchildren are going to be left with a dozen species of birds that can adapt to life in the inner city. This is unreality because the future is not necessarily so bleak. We do have all sorts of environmental problems, but they're problems that can be addressed if we will open our eyes and perceive them as they are, and open our eyes to potential solutions and put the necessary processes in place to make those solutions become reality.

No little bird that we thrill to see, no one of us, no species of bird nor our own human species, no island or continent on this earth, nor the earth itself nor the cosmos, is permanent. All is transient; all will eventually pass on. Shunryu Suzuki has commented that acceptance of the pervasiveness of change is attainment of Nirvana. Many of us grieve upon glimpsing this truth, and then we resist it and go into mourning. Our resistance is the basis of our suffering.

Do we, then, slip into apathy? Do we decide that our lives are not worth living, or that the innumerable species of wise and beautiful living creatures on this earth are not worth saving?

In an undisciplined state of mind, such despair is certainly possible. But this is born of bad karma, born of an illusion that thinks nothing worthwhile unless it is eternal. If we can but wake up, and see reality as it is, we will see that now is the only moment that matters.

This does not mean we must be unflaggingly optimistic!

Do you know the difference between optimism and apathy?

Optimism sees beauty and vows to protect it. Apathy sees beauty and walks away untouched.

Do you know the difference between pessimism and apathy?

Pessimism sees a danger and vows to attack it. Apathy sees a danger and concedes without a fight.

Apathy is uninvolved.

Do you know the difference between involvement and attachment?

Involvement recognizes the importance of certain results in the world and sacrifices ego for the furtherance of those outcomes.

Attachment sees certain results in the world as desirable and sees success or failure in achieving those results as a reflection of ego.

Do you know the difference between grieving and mourning?

Grieving sees a loss or threatened loss and focuses on ways in which loss might be stemmed or reversed. Differently said, grieving recognizes and remains aware of loss, without feeling hopeless or defeated. Mourning sees only the loss, without seeking relief. Mourning recognizes and remains aware of, and is debilitated by, the sense of loss.

What makes people curmudgeonly is the inability (or unwillingness) to see the difference between what is, and what he or she thinks should be. What makes a person apathetic is the inability to tell the difference between what is now, and what might be.

One can easily get grumpy when seeing wonderful habitat for birds and other wildlife being destroyed for parking lots, houses and strip malls. That attitude is not, in and of itself, inappropriate. But if one gets stuck in grumpiness and negativity, the result is a curmudgeon and nothing more. We can, instead, lobby for better planning and zoning that takes the needs of wildlife into account, shifting the focus. That way, we can avoid slipping from curmudgeonry into apathy.

Slipping in and out of optimism and pessimism can become almost like breathing—a meditation in and of itself. Breathe in pessimism; breathe out optimism.

When grounded in reality, there are no guarantees on

either optimism or pessimism. We currently face a choice of which many people are quite unaware. We are now choosing, bit by bit, between preserving a living planet and creating a dead, synthetic planet. To make a fully conscious choice requires broadening our viewpoints and seeing issues in their full complexity.

We need both optimism and pessimism. Only the pessimistic vision of the last Resplendent Quetzal, Robin, or Starling, can shock us back into optimistic determination to not let it go that way!

In New Mexico, water use is an extremely important environmental and economic issue. Many people have been putting this into a very simple context. A hugely complex issue became known as the silvery minnow issue, just because this was the species most immediately endangered by water shortages. The mayor of Albuquerque further flattened the problem by asking if we were going to take the water out of our children's mouths and give it to a little fish. Of course, it really wasn't a question of children versus minnows. It was (and is) a question of conscious use of water and all of the multiple ways that water is needed. It's needed for farming, for human consumption, and for the river—not just for the minnow, but for all of the other fishes and plants that live along the river and the bosque and the birds and animals that depend on the bosque. A whole ecosystem involves people and plants and animals.

The question is, are we going to preserve an ecosystem that has value for humans, or are we going to say that people need all the water and so we'll put it in a pipeline and let the river go dead? That's really the big picture we need to see. By all of our little daily choices we are creating a larger future, and we're making a choice between an engineered planet and a living, breathing planet.

This is a fundamental choice. Some people might prefer to live on an engineered planet where the entire planet is enclosed in a atmospherically-regulated plastic bubble where there are no non-human living creatures. There may be no difference between land and ocean because we've decided that it's all about utilitarian value and how we can engineer it to sustain several thousand billion people. Such an evolutionary choice is not likely to succeed. Any attempt at total planetary engineering is likely to collapse under its own weight and lack of wisdom.

In the long run, birds are much more likely to inherit this planet than we are. And so our interest in preserving a habitat sustaining bird life should be as much an interest as preserving a habitat that will sustain human life. Successfully creating a planet that has only ourselves on it is unlikely. Any attempt to do that is folly and ultimately shows a lack of wisdom. A useful view for us is to look at the wisdom of non-human animals, and see the lack of this sort of "conquer the planet" mentality, that they live within systems that sustain themselves through diversity, not through dominance by any one life form.

Consider predatory birds—ravens, as an example. They're notorious for going around raiding the nests of other birds. They got all the baby Scaled Quails in our Santa Fe yard one year. They raided the nest and ate the eggs before the little quails could hatch. But what typically happens when ravens become too successful and there aren't enough little birds with nests to sustain them, then their population crashes and the populations of quail and jays and other birds that ravens victimize rebound for a time. This is of course an oversimplification, as ravens are in fact generalists who subsist on many things other than eggs and baby birds. But the point is that there's a balance, however rough and uneven it may appear, such that no one species is able to operate at the expense of others for very long. Their very success that defeats them. So we must consider what could also happen to humans. If we successfully displace all other life on the planet, it will not work to our benefit.

Beyond all considerations of human pragmatics, though, it is appropriate for us to realize that this is not a contest between avian and human survival. The outcome will likely be either win/win or lose/lose for both. If the demise of the miner's canary goes unheeded, both perish and it matters not who takes the last breath.

From an evolutionary perspective, we must consider the possibility that our species, *Homo sapiens*, is fatally flawed. Our unique variety of intelligence may be more a matter of cleverness than of wisdom and we may find ourselves unable to adapt to the environment we are creating for ourselves. From a spiritual perspective, it is incumbent upon us to consider this closely, and to work intently at helping our species find a place of harmony and equilibrium with the cosmos—if, indeed, this is possible for us. This is a matter of choice. We must become fully conscious of what is involved. We must "wake up."

If we can see and accept that the death of a chickadee is not the death of the species, and that even the death of our own species will not be the end of living beings, then we can be released from suffering. To release our individual selfhood is to be washed in the flow of all life, beyond which no creature can see. Surrendering to our transient nature, we can take meaningful action in the present moment.

One of the biggest impediments we face, in attempting to take meaningful action, is anger. But succumbing to anger leads to defeat. The Dalai Lama urges us to understand our enemies rather than attacking them, for it is through understanding that we find the greatest possibility of doing good, for all concerned. Understanding must come in the present moment.

Now.

Now is the time to shake up the karma of the future, the time to strive for life. Now is the time to take a small action that will have great consequences. Perhaps most important of all, now is the time for us to find our personal and collective courage to take appropriate actions even if they seem, at first glance, futile.

Now is the time to think about recycling, about composting and growing at least some of our own food, about eating organic and lower on the food chain, about saying something that will change someone's attitude, about donating time or money to a worthwhile cause, about researching ways of reducing our carbon footprint, about doing something to save a bit of wild habitat or assist an endangered species.

Now is the time to be in this moment.

Now might be a good time to go Zen birding.

ON THE IMPORTANCE OF CAPITALIZING BIRD NAMES

If I saw a white-tailed tropicbird, I may either have seen a White-tailed Tropicbird or a Red-billed Tropicbird; if I saw a red-billed tropicbird, I may either have seen a Red-tailed Tropicbird or a Red-billed Tropicbird; it is only if I saw a tropicbird both white-tailed and red-billed that I can confidently say I saw a Red-billed Tropicbird.

(David, March 20, 2002, Kilauea Point National Wildlife Refuge, Kauai HI)

ABOUT THE AUTHORS

David M. White, Ph.D.

David wrote *Zen Birding* from a passion for his daily birding walks as well as leadership in birding organizations. He received his Ph.D. in Anthropology from Southern Methodist University in 1977. Through his consulting firm, Applied Cultural Dynamics, David conducted ethnohistorical studies for the National Park Service, American Indian tribes, and other clients.

His lifelong passion for birding, combined with an anthropological point-of-view, give a unique perspective on the different cultural approaches birders bring to their activity. His involvement with the Audubon Society (Los Angeles and Santa Fe chapters) as a board member and field trip leader provided the direct experience of interacting with a broad range of people with diverse interests in birding. His interest in Buddhism and eastern thought brought him to see birds not as objects to be pursued and counted, but rather as sentient beings with whom we share the planet.

Susan M. Guyette, Ph.D.

Susan is Métis, an ethnic background of Micmac Indian and Acadian French heritage. She received a Ph.D. in Anthropology from Southern Methodist University in 1975 and a Masters Degree in Urban and Regional Planning in 1986. Her work with Native American communities focuses on cultural preservation, sustainable tourism, and culturally-based economic development. Recovery from Multiple

Chemical Sensitivities (MCS), after being chemically injured in 1998 by pesticide, led her to a passion for environmental issues. She has written three books previously: *Planning for Balanced Development, Issues for the Future of American Indian Studies*, and *Community-Based Research*. She is a student of Vipassana Buddhism.

GRATITUDES

David:

To Randolph, who told me that God is more easily found on the banks of a creek than sitting on a hard church pew;
To Myrtle, and Richard, who taught me serenity;
To Marcella, who taught me to see beauty;
To Marvin, who taught me discipline;
To Agnes, who taught me to ask questions;
To Curtis, who taught me to explore and observe;
To Susan, who encouraged me to write; and
To Rick, who knew the writing would happen on its own schedule.

Susan:

The journey of *Zen Birding* took many unexpected turns. To those who helped David and me along the way, my gratitude is large. Throughout this book, a path of determination led to the appreciation of being in life's moment, for one never knows how many moments there will be. In a true fight for life, David's passion for birding and the preservation of habitat supported his writing process through two years of cancer treatment. My gratitude to David and to his passion for the environment expands every day.

New Mexico Audubon encouraged the completion of this book and recognized David's contribution as Vice President of the Sangre de Cristo chapter of the Audubon Society. I am particularly grateful to New Mexico President Tom Jervis and Sangre de Cristo President Tom Taylor for their confidence in the book and for creating the David White Memorial Fund for Habitat Conservation.

First, I would like to thank Joan Chernock for transforming an assorted pile of notes and flagged passages on handwritten birding notebooks into an electronic file – the beginnings of

ZEBI, as *Zen Birding* came to be fondly called. Her support-iveness helped us launch this project.

Loving friends, Lee Tayloe, Carol Roberts, Craig Conley, Betsy and Steve Pierce, helped us reach Seattle from Santa Fe to secure medical support for David.

My heartfelt thanks to the extraordinary medical team in Seattle who provided the very best encouragement and treatment. Drs. Keith Eaton, Jason Rockhill, Robin Chun, and Daniel Silbergeld, along with Providence Hospice staff Mary Roy, Twila Forbes, Angela Lim, and Kevin Read, heightened David's encouragement with their extraordinary care.

David's mother, Marcella, his brother Rick White and sister-in-law Kristina extended daily loving kindness and support to keep this book moving as a project of hope for environmental awareness.

My family's encouragement enabled me to turn grief into the creativity needed to complete this book. Thank you – Mona St. Jean, Esther Bell, Patricia Phillips, Albertine and Bob Phillips, and Lorraine Jacques.

My son, Austin Spafford, gave love and care-giving assistance, keeping us positive through the treatment process, to the end of David's life. His friend, Mike Durkin provided loving and gentle care-giving. My hope for their generation is an enhanced connection to the environment through this book.

As an agent, Sammie Justensen persisted to find a publisher in difficult economic times. John Hunt, owner of O-Books, perceived the wisdom and potential of *Zen Birding's* themes.

Gratitude is extended to Rob Jordan for his deep friendship, editing assistance, and encouragement to persist through the publication process. Doug Trent (Focus Tours) assisted with comments. Cathryn Kasper brought editing assistance to the finish line.

Thank you, thank you, all.

REFERENCES

Preface

Zen master Bong Soo Han, in *Zen in the Martial Arts*, Joe Hyams, editor. N.Y: Bantam Books, 1979.

Introduction

Snetsinger, Phoebe. *Birding on Borrowed Time*. Colorado Springs, CO: American Birding Association, 2003.

Suzuki, Shunryo. *Zen Mind, Beginner's Mind*. New York: Weatherhill, 1970.

Hanh, Thich Nhat Hanh. *Teachings on Love*. In, The Thich Nhat Hanh Collection. New York: One Spirit, 2004.

Zenrin in *A Little Book of Zen*, Katherine Kim, editor. Kansas City, MO: Andrews McMeel Publishing, 1998.

Chapter 1

Koeppel, Dan. *To See Every Bird on Earth*. New York: Penguin Group, 2005.

Merton, Thomas, *Zen and the Birds of Appetite*. New York: New Directions Books, 1968.

Nietzsche, Friedrich. *Beyond Good and Evil*. In, *The Selected Writings of Frederich Nietzsche*. Radford, VA: Wilder Publications, 2008.

Obmascik, Mark. *The Big Year: A Tale of Man, Nature and Fowl Obsession*. New York: Free Press, 2004.

Chapter 2

Abram, David. *The Spell of the Sensuous*. New York: Vintage Books, 1997.

Burns, Jim. "Time, Rock, and the River." *Birding* 34(2):204-206, 2002.

Dillard, Annie. *Pilgrim at Tinker Creek*. New York: Harper's

Magazine Press, 1974.

Dunne, Pete. *The Feather Quest*. Boston: First Mariner Books, 1999.

Dunne, Pete. *Pete Dunne on Bird Watching*. Boston: Houghton Mifflin Company, 2003.

Jarvis, E.D., O. Güntürkün, L. Bruce, A. Csillag, H. Karten, W. Kuenzel, L. Medina, G. Paxinos, D. J. Perkel, T. Shimizu, G. Striedter, M. Wild, G. F. Ball, J. Dugas-Ford, S. Durand, G. Hough, S. Husband, L. Kubikova, D. Lee, C.V. Mello, A. Powers, C. Siang, T.V. Smulders, K. Wada, S.A. White, K. Yamamoto, J. Yu, A. Reiner, and A. B. Butler. "Avian Brains and a New Understanding of Vertebrate Brain Evolution." *Nature Reviews Neuroscience* 6:151-159, 2005.

Kornfield, Jack. *A Path With Heart*. New York: Bantam Books, 1993.

Knudson, E. "Instructed Learning in the Auditory Localization Pathway of the Barn Owl." *Nature* 417:322-328, 2002.

Rattenborg, N.C., S.L. Lima, and C.J. Amlaner. "Half-awake to the Risk of Predation." *Nature* 397:397, 1999.

Sudo, Philip, *Zen Sex*. New York: Harper San Francisco, 2000.

Chapter 3

Bhante Henepola Gunaratana, *Mindfullness in Plain English*. Boston: Wisdom Publications, 2002.

Kaufman, Kenn. *Kingbird Highway*. New York: Mifflin, 1997.

Smith, Jean. *The Beginner's Guide to Zen Buddhism*. New York: Bell Tower, 2000.

Sumedho, Ajahn. *Teachings of a Buddhist Monk*. Srilanka: Buddhist Publishing Group, 1995.

Chapter 4

Dogen, *Moon in a Dewdrop*, Kazuaki Tanahashi (ed.). San Francisco: North Point Press, 1985.

Ogburn, Charlton. *The Adventure of Birds*. New York: William Morrow, 1975.

Nabhan, Gary Paul. *Cultures of Habitat*. Washington, D.C.: Counterpoint, 1997.

Thich Naht Hahn. *No Death, Nor Fear: Comforting Wisdom for Life*. New York: Penguin Putnam, 1985.

Chapter 5

American Birding Association. *Big Day Report* (Supplement to *Birding*, Vol. 34 No.3), 2001.

Baker, Beth. "Rx Nature," *Nature Conservancy Magazine*, 52(4): 88, 2002.

Berry, Wendell. *Life is a Miracle: An Essay Against Modern Superstition*. Washington, D.C.: Counterpoint, 2000.

Cajete, Gregory. *Native Science: Natural Laws of Interdependence*. Santa Fe, NM: Clear Light Publishers, 2000.

McKibben, Bill. *The End of Nature*. New York: Anchor Books, Doubleday, 1990.

Louv, Richard. *Last Child in the Woods*. Chapel Hill, NC: Algonquin Books, 2005

Obmascik, Mark. *The Big Year: A Tale of Man, Nature and Fowl Obsession*. New York: Free Press, 2004.

Peterson, Roger Tory. *All Things Reconsidered: My Birding Adventures*. New York: Houghton Mifflin, 2006.

Chapter 7

Kornfield, Jack. *A Path With Heart*. New York: Bantam Books, 1993.

Ogburn, Charlton. *The Adventure of Birds*. New York: William Morrow, 1975.

Nabhan, Gary Paul. *Cultures of Habitat*. Washington, D.C.: Counterpoint, 1997.

Conclusion

His Holiness, the IVth Dalai Lama. Nobel Peace Prize Lecture. 1989.

Snelling, John. *The Elements of Buddhism*. Rockport, MA: Element Books, 1992.

Tennant, Alan. *On the Wing: To the Edge of the Earth with the Peregrine Falcon*. New York: Alfred Knopf, 2004.

Wendell Berry. *Life is a Miracle: An Essay Against Modern Superstition*. Washington, D.C.: Counterpoint, 2000.

BOOKS

O is a symbol of the world, of oneness and unity. In different cultures it also means the "eye," symbolizing knowledge and insight. We aim to publish books that are accessible, constructive and that challenge accepted opinion, both that of academia and the "moral majority."

Our books are available in all good English language bookstores worldwide. If you don't see the book on the shelves ask the bookstore to order it for you, quoting the ISBN number and title. Alternatively you can order online (all major online retail sites carry our titles) or contact the distributor in the relevant country, listed on the copyright page.

See our website **www.o-books.net** for a full list of over 500 titles, growing by 100 a year.

And tune in to myspiritradio.com for our book review radio show, hosted by June-Elleni Laine, where you can listen to the authors discussing their books.